COLLEGE BOUND

COLLEGE BOUND

The Student's Handbook For Getting Ready, Moving In, and Succeeding On Campus

Evelyn Kaye and Janet Gardner

College Entrance Examination Board, New York

To Allan and Christopher,
who were freshmen at Columbia and Cambridge
a very long time ago

In all of its book publishing activities the College Board endeavors to present the works of authors who are well qualified to write with authority on the subject at hand, and to present accurate and timely information. However, the opinions, interpretations, and conclusions of the authors are their own and do not necessarily represent those of the College Board; nothing contained herein should be assumed to represent an official position of the College Board, or any of its members.

Copies of this book may be ordered from College Board Publications, Box 886, New York, New York 10101-0886. The price is $9.95.

Editorial inquiries concerning this book should be directed to Editorial Office, The College Board, 45 Columbus Avenue, New York, New York 10023-6992.

The College Board, Scholastic Aptitude Test, SAT, and the acorn logo are registered trademarks of the College Entrance Examination Board. Library of Congress Catalog Number: 88-071230

ISBN: 0-87447-3047
Printed in the United States of America.

9 8 7 6 5 4 3 2 1

Contents

3   *What Do I Need to Take?*   25

6 *The First Few Days* **91**

7 *Who Can Answer My Questions?* **105**

𝟪 *Settling In*   **117**

𝟫 *Learning the Academic Ropes*   **135**

Acknowledgments

This book represents the accumulated wisdom and experience of hundreds of people who know what they're talking about.

We listened to students about to make the transition from high school to college. We interviewed college freshmen and other undergraduates about how they cope. We sent questionnaires to high school guidance counselors and deans of admissions at colleges and universities around the country.

We really want to thank the many people who contributed to this book—so we're going to list them all. Their insight and suggestions were extraordinarily helpful.

Our thanks to high school counselors at: Watchung Hills Regional High School, Warren, New Jersey; Albert Einstein High School, Kensington, Maryland; St. Mark's High School, Wilmington, Delaware; Strake Jesuit College Preparatory School, Houston, Texas; Cherry Creek High School, Englewood, Colorado; Los Angeles Unified School District, Los Angeles, California; the Bush School, Seattle, Washington; Baltimore City Schools, Baltimore, Maryland; and the New York City Board of Education.

Our thanks to admission officers at: University of California at Berkeley; Stanford University; Yale University; University of Delaware; Howard University; University of Miami; Emory University; Northwestern University; Grinnell College; Loyola University; Clark

University; Harvard and Radcliffe Universities; Tufts University; University of Michigan; Dartmouth College; Princeton University; University of New Mexico; Cornell University; New York University; Vassar College; Duke University; Kent State University; University of Tulsa; Lewis and Clark College; Carnegie-Mellon University; Drexel University; Haverford College; Brown University; Rice University; Bennington College; University of Virginia; Evergreen State College; Columbia University; Pennsylvania State University; Washington State University; University of Texas; Colorado State University; Kenyon College; Syracuse University; Southern Methodist University; Oberlin College; University of Nebraska; University of California at Los Angeles; Ohio State University; Hood College; University of Mississippi; Elon College; Franklin and Marshall College; Wellesley College; Wesleyan University; University of Rochester; University of Pennsylvania; Bowdoin College; University of Hawaii; Ramapo College; University of Chicago; Villanova University; University of Vermont; Middlebury College; Georgetown University; University of Wisconsin; and Manhattanville College.

Some of the best advice came from those in the front lines—the students. A special thank-you to: Andrew Gardner, Elisabeth Gardner, Katrina Sarson, David Sarson, Lisa Harrington, David Gibbon, Brian Hoffman, Jenny Libien, Joshua M. David, Peter Doherty, Judith Gruen, Ilana Feldman, Mitchell Berman, John Capen, Cythia Hiller, and Susanna Bjorkman.

Also, thanks to: Will Garrett, Michael Gutwirth, Jeanne Dobkin, Oliver Sadeh, Jay Violet, Marcia Whitaker, Belinda Hahn, Lisa Chang, Douglas Schlosser, Anna Jane Harrison, Natasha Levine, Debra Cominsky, Josh Freed, Rheta Brown, Manuel Espinoza, Gerard Seaver, Naomi Ying, Winston R. Brown, Phillip O'Riordan, Andrea Orlick, Libby Cavanagh, Kim Lee Cheung, Peter Gerson, Dolores Suarez, Louisa Hyde,

Gretchen Ericsonn, Martha Ashe, Robert Robinson, Carole Bradley, Enrique Cruz, Lin Lee, Penny Ruttenberg, and Jennifer Vonschreiber.

We are grateful to the mothers and fathers who shared with us the ups and downs of packing their offspring off to college. A warm vote of thanks to our agent, Carole Abel, who, with two college-age sons, empathized enthusiastically with this book idea. And finally, our sincere thanks to our editor, Carolyn Trager, for her support and encouragement.

1

Getting Organized
For College

Congratulations! You've received your acceptance letters, decided where to enroll, sent in your deposit, and soon you'll be going away to college! You're going to be living on your own.

This is very different from going away to summer camp or spending a week with relatives at the seashore. You're at the beginning of grown-up life. When you think about it, you probably feel both exhilarated and terrified. As one high school senior put it, "I can't separate the excitement from the apprehension. I'm glad to be going, but I'm worried underneath."

You've probably been dreaming about going for a long time. You made it through the PSAT/NMSQTs, the SATs, and the Achievement Tests. You filled out stacks of forms and perfected your application essay so that the admission committee recognized your unique qualities. You persuaded the teachers who know you and your abilities best to write your recommendations. You survived stomach-churning interviews in which you managed to express a passionate desire to attend that particular school. You visited bustling city and tranquil tree-lined campuses trying to make rational distinctions between the small private college and the multicampus state university. Did all the kids look too preppy? Too artsy? Did anybody look like somebody you could talk to? You spent hours on the phone with your friends analyzing what they thought and what you thought and what they were doing and what you were doing and why. Of course, your parents had their own ideas, and your high school counselor gave you yet another perspective.

Perhaps you began to wonder if you'd get in anywhere. You can still remember the moment of ecstasy when you opened a letter of acceptance. You'd like to forget the agony of waiting, and, perhaps, the pain of a skinny rejection letter. But now you can look back at everything you've accomplished. You should be feeling pretty proud of yourself. Hold on to that feeling! It will help you in those moments when you're overwhelmed by thoughts about taking off for college.

The Big Picture

Although this is probably one of the biggest moments in your life, it may be useful to remember that you are one student going off to one college. In 1988, nearly seven million full-time students enrolled in colleges and universities across the country. You are becoming part of a long tradition of higher education in the United States. If you haven't been told already, someone is sure to point out that going to college is both a privilege and a responsibility.

The 1986 Carnegie Foundation report, "College: The Undergraduate Experience in America," concluded that "The aim of the undergraduate experience is not only to prepare the young to be productive, but also to enable them to live with dignity and purpose; not only to generate new knowledge, but to channel that knowledge to humane ends; not merely to study government, but to shape a citizenry that can promote the public good."

These highfalutin' ideas may not be the first thing you think of when your alarm goes off at seven in the morning, but they are what college is all about.

What's Different About College?

You're going to have lots of new experiences and, at the beginning, maybe a touch of old-fashioned homesickness. At college, you'll be in charge. You'll manage your money. You'll arrange your class schedule, decide when to study and when to socialize. You'll find out if you can build a loft in your dorm room. You'll get the telephone number of the best pizza place that delivers. If you don't feel good, you'll get yourself over to Student Health Services.

You'll face what seems at first to be an unending stream of chores and choices. Nobody will remind you to get up, to go to class, to do your laundry, to return your library books. Nobody will care if you wear the same shirt for two weeks, skip meals, and party five nights a week. The decisions are yours, even though parents and friends are only a phone call away.

College is a new ball game in which all the rookie players start out together and no one's too sure of the rules. The competition can be pretty rough. You may have been editor of your high school paper, but so were thirteen other students in your freshman English class. Said one college counselor at the University of Wisconsin: "If you've been a good student in high school, at college you'll find that everyone's been a good student in high school. You may not get straight A's again."

Or, you may be challenged to work harder than you ever have been before, become the founding editor of a new literary magazine, and graduate summa cum laude!

Learning the Rules

Up to now, if you're like most teenagers, your behavior has been guided by rules established by parents and teachers. Your folks told you if you could have a party, told you there was to be no alcohol, and made it clear when the party would be over. At school functions, teachers kept an eye on what was happening.

If you chose to ignore the rules, chances were that you got into trouble.

In some important ways, those days are over. If you want to have a party at college, you can have one. In most schools no chaperones will be assigned, and nobody will tell your friends that it's time to go home. Colleges do have rules; but as an adult you are expected to abide by them without constant monitoring.

Maybe this is exactly what you want. You and your parents have different ideas about behavior. You think your high school treated you like a first grader. Or perhaps you've always felt comfortable knowing what the boundaries are, and feel threatened by the freedom of college life.

At college, you may find yourself facing questions you never had to ask yourself before. How do you feel about partying? About drinking? About drugs? About sex? These are complex questions, and it's a good sign if you're feeling anxious about them because your answers can have serious, long-term consequences.

Colleges make their rules clear and enforce them with sanctions that range from suspension to expulsion. Also, there are state and federal laws that apply to you. Making mistakes with a small "m"—like piercing three holes in your left ear, or painting your room black, or rarely getting up before noon—is part of growing up. However, with a modicum of forethought and maturity, you should be able to avoid making mistakes with a capital "M."

Even if you see getting away from home as a great escape, your first chance to break loose, any sophomore will tell you to keep your cool, especially in the excitement of the first few weeks.

Gearing Up

If you're like the students we know, you're getting worried and doing nothing. You know you ought to be making lists, shopping, calling your roommate if your college has given you his or her name, cleaning out your room, and packing up. But somehow you just can't get going. There are too many details, too much to get organized.

Your father wants you to price computers; your mother says you need shoes, you don't own a parka and you're going to school in Maine; you haven't been to the dentist since a year ago December; your grandmother in Florida wants to see you; and you're determined to buy contact lenses and get used to them before you take off. How are you going to get it all done?

If panic is paralyzing you, this book will help you get moving. In it you will find everything you need to know before you go and once you get there.

Firsthand Advice

This book answers many questions that you have about going off to college—and some you may not have thought of yet. Scores of students, parents, and high school and college counselors shared their experience

with us about what you really need to take with you
and what you can skip; what you should worry about
and what you shouldn't; which decisions have to be
made immediately and which can wait until you settle
into your college routine. Based on their accumulated
knowledge and our hands-on experience as parents of
four college-age kids, this book is your guide to a
trouble-free transition from high school to college.

How to Use this Book

Every graduating senior has worries about the first
weeks of college. When we asked, "What are you most
worried about?," we always got an answer—and usually a long one! Only one student said, "What? Me
worry?" So take heart: You have lots of company.

We've organized this book to follow the time frame
you'll probably use as you get ready and go off to college. If you look through these pages, you'll know what
to expect.

- First Steps: From early orientation to getting your
  technical skills and your body in shape.
- What to Take with You: Lists, lists, lists—of clothing, furnishings, and books—plus luggage and packing tips.
- Money Matters: Deciding what you will pay and
  what your parents will pay; keeping track of expenses; whether you'll need to get a job.
- College Countdown: Starting four weeks before
  school begins, details of what you have to get done
  and when.
- First Days on Campus: Moving in without tears;

enjoying freshman orientation; getting to know your roommate(s); and finding your way around.

- Finding the Answers: A resource list of people who can answer your questions about finances, housing, courses, health, and campus activities.
- Settling In: Coping with Freshman Shock and homesickness; new faces and new freedoms.
- Academic Aspects: Choosing your courses; finding your study style; learning your way around the libraries; managing your time.

And, to help you keep track of your jam-packed college days, we've provided a personal address book for all the new friends you're going to make. Plus, for next year, when you are a sophisticated sophomore, there's a section for you to write down what you've left behind and where you left it.

Good-byes

While you can schedule packing up, moving in, and settling down, feelings are much less easily organized.

It's sad to think about saying good-bye to special friends—especially girlfriends and boyfriends. This is tough, no question. You want to be loyal, and yet you know you shouldn't close yourself off and miss out on one of the most significant aspects of college life— meeting new people.

Andrea, a Stanford student, spent her freshman year traveling to Los Angeles almost every weekend to visit her boyfriend at UCLA. "We agreed I'd do this," she said, "but looking back, I realize it was a big mistake because I cut myself off just when I should have been getting to know my classmates. And then he found a girlfriend in Los Angeles. We broke up and I had a really unhappy time."

The students to whom we've talked about this sensitive and sometimes painful problem agree that there's less anxiety if you can agree to let go. Some couples survive a separation and some don't.

"Those promises of eternal fidelity put enormous pressure on both of you when you're in college," said Jeff, who watched his roommate go through the long, drawn-out demise of a high school romance.

You're saying good-bye to your family, as well. You're anticipating life on your own without your mom reminding you to clean up your room and your dad pointing out that you haven't washed the car. At the same time, you know you're going to miss everybody.

Your family has the same mixed feelings. They're proud of you. They hope you do well. They want you to be happy. But they may find it hard to back off—after all, they've had you around for seventeen years or so, and they've gotten used to you. It's strange for parents to look at your empty chair at dinner. The bathroom is distressingly neat. The phone hardly ever rings. The peanut butter lasts forever.

You won't see any of this, but you should think about it. Most parents try not to interfere, but it's hard after a lifetime of being in charge. It may take your mother a while to stop asking if you've changed your sheets, but she will. As you settle in and demonstrate that you can manage on your own, your parents will step back. But in the beginning parents aren't the only people who have to be patient. They have to alter their pattern of parenting. It may take some time, so try to be understanding.

"I missed Cindy terribly for the first couple of months," said her mother. "I actually cried when I looked at her room. Then she came home for Thanksgiving and while it was wonderful I could see that she was doing just fine on her own and couldn't wait to get back. I realized I'd done a good job and though I still missed her it was okay."

A clinical psychologist at the University of Notre Dame said, "Some students are just not prepared to live independently. They are uncomfortable making simple decisions like what to do when they're hungry and the school cafeteria is closed." One college dorm counselor noted that parents who call and visit too frequently often create unhappiness, giving kids the message that they can't manage on their own.

His advice to parents is: "Your freshman needs to know you're there, but it's better to do too little than too much." Finding the right balance for a family takes time, so bear this in mind if your parents seem over-anxious at first.

Stay Cool!

Do you wake up in the middle of the night convinced that you will never get your stuff together in time? Does your mother wonder aloud how you are ever going to manage on your own when you've forgotten to pick up your clothes from the cleaners for the third day in a row? Have you started making lists but failed to cross off one single thing?

Relax. Everybody suffers from precollege jitters. If you're like the students we know, you're worried about what kind of stuff you need. How big is the room? Do they give you a pillow? Will you need a computer? Can you hang posters? Does everybody have a telephone? Should you bring your bike? What if you forget something?

Everyone forgets something. Unless you are going to be a freshman at Outer Mongolia State where the mail comes in by yak once a month, don't panic. Wherever you go there will be stores nearby to sell you batteries for your Walkman and virtually everything else you can think of. Your parents will be glad to send you the down jacket you left in the hall closet. And you can pick up your snorkel when you go home for Thanksgiving.

This book is designed to help you, the about-to-be college freshman, get organized before you have to get going and get settled in once you're there. Go through these pages and think about what you really need and what you can skip.

To get rid of that overwhelmed feeling, just take the first step. If you can cross one item off your list, you'll feel light-years better—and so will your parents. And you'll find that you can move on to the next item, and the next. It may be hard to believe, but you *will* get everything done before you take off.

2

First Steps

From Senior to Freshman

One December day, a student in Washington, D.C., was delighted to receive an envelope of acceptance material from Wesleyan University, including a sticker for her car. "But most of my friends hadn't applied early," she said, "so they were still sweating it out. I didn't dare put the sticker on the back window until the end of April, when everybody knew where they were going."

Like most seniors, you probably didn't find out where you'd been accepted until April. After you finished dancing around the kitchen, calling your friends and your grandmother, and hugging your parents, you began to come down to earth. You'd thought getting in to college would solve all your problems: Now you realize that you have a whole new bunch of questions! We hope you got your first choice, but even if you didn't or were wait-listed, you know by now which colleges offered you admission.

Were you accepted by more than one college? Are you still set on your first choice? What is the deadline for letting each school know of your decision? Can you attend an early orientation program to introduce you to college life?

Don't throw the acceptance materials under your bed thinking, "I'll check these out later." Get the necessary forms out and fees paid on schedule.

Avoiding Senior Slump

Parents hear rumors about it, teachers warn against its insidious effect, but most students say it's a phenomenon blown out of all proportion.

We're talking about Senior Slump—that tricky time when your mind is more on college than high school. Some people think that the moment a high school senior is accepted to college, the brain turns to mush and even the most responsible student stops working and is transformed into a wild party animal. The reality is that there *are* cases of Senior Slump, but not every graduating senior succumbs to the epidemic.

Some students actually work harder during senior year. Jenny said that her grades got better. "The University of Pennsylvania had accepted me and I just felt like a good student. Senior Slump did hit some people, but they were the people who had Junior Slump, too."

Some students actually learn better with the pressure off, and may even take extra courses in subjects that particularly interest them. But some students do poop out, cutting classes and failing to hand in papers.

In Josh's private school, second semester seniors are not required to take finals. "We still had to hand in papers and stuff," he said, "but Senior Slump was a definite factor because, after April, everybody's head was in college."

The truth is that teachers and parents probably *over*estimate—and students *under*estimate—the effects of Senior Slump. Junior year and the beginning of senior year in high school score high on the stress scale, and a let-up is understandable. But before you find yourself cutting morning classes to hang out with your friends and compare notes about colleges, reread your letter of acceptance. Your college expects you to maintain the level of achievement that got you accepted in the first place. Failing to complete graduation requirements means that you may have to go to summer school or make up the credits during your freshman year.

A high school counselor in Ohio said, "Some students tend to get carried away by the anticipation of going to college. And of course there are all the special senior activities—the senior play, the prom, the yearbook, the honors assembly—which are good excuses for letting things slide. We try to keep an eye out for students who aren't meeting their responsibilities. Generally, most students are pretty good about it."

So while you may think your teachers and parents are paranoid about Senior Slump, it doesn't take a genius to figure out that goofing off may be hazardous to your collegiate health.

Early Orientation

Some colleges offer brief early orientation programs to students who've been accepted. Don't confuse early orientation with regular freshman orientation, which takes place a few days before the sophomores, juniors, and seniors arrive on campus for the opening of school.

"When you go to early orientation, it's very different from going for an interview," said Naomi, now a law student at the University of Virginia. "The first time around, you're nervous, trying to make the right impression. When you go back, they're trying to make an impression on *you* so that you'll decide to come."

Everyone we spoke to who attended these early introductory programs found them extremely helpful and reassuring. The school has accepted you, wants you to come, and is trying to present itself in the best possible light. Besides being a real blast, these introductory sessions are carefully planned to answer many of your questions about college life. They usually take a couple of days, and in that time you'll meet a whole bunch of fellow students, some professors and deans, and other members of the college administration. Do go, if you can find the time and the money.

Brian, a freshman at the University of Rochester, attended a three-day program in the spring of his senior year. "The great thing about my visit was that it made me feel I was no longer an outsider looking in. I stayed with a couple of really nice guys and met a lot of other freshmen. I went to some classes. I found the dorm I wanted to be in. It was super! I'm totally psyched!"

Brian had pre-registered for a special self-contained residential hall where a small group of students and teachers all live and study together. But he changed his mind. "I found out that there were scheduling problems, that I didn't want to limit myself. Also, I thought one of the professors was lousy," he said frankly.

These early visits help you plan for September. You can get a head start on finding your way around, check out the sports facilities, and sample the food in the dining hall.

Kim was debating between Northwestern in Evanston, Illinois, and an East Coast university. Orientation weekend in Evanston convinced her that Northwestern was the place for her. "I couldn't visit before I applied, so I didn't know how beautiful it was, right on the lake. The theater facilities were even better than I'd imagined."

There can be some hazards, though. At her early orientation, Libby met a freshman who also planned to go out for crew, and the two girls asked to room together. "It did make me feel good to know who my roommate was going to be; however, once we lived together it turned out we didn't have all that much in common after all. Looking back, I might have been better off with the luck of the draw. Or maybe not!"

Some parents accompany their children to early orientation. If yours do, you may not see much of them because they'll be busy with their own activities such as attending a seminar on finances, listening to a speech by the college president, or participating in a discussion on the psychological and social aspects of campus life. Said the father of an Ohio freshman: "I liked being told not to panic if we got a lot of phone calls from Matthew, and also not to panic if he never called at all. We didn't make an issue about keeping in touch, and as it turns out, we talk to him about once a week."

Video Visits

A new wrinkle in college marketing is the video visit. Instead of going to the campus, the campus comes to you through videos describing programs and facilities.

Your high school guidance counselor may be able to get these for you. For example, Learning Resources Network is a program in which over 1,400 high schools across the country participate. If your high school isn't a member, you can call 1-800-CALL-LRN to buy a video. For a small fee you will receive a 10-to-15 minute presentation from a list of colleges in more than 30 states. There are also other companies that provide similar services.

First Things First

June turns into July and July slips into August and suddenly you're leaving the day after tomorrow. Only Superman can do everything faster than a speeding bullet: You don't have enough time to do it all in a couple of days. Your parents keep trying to tell you this—and any college sophomore will admit, albeit unwillingly, that they were right. Let's take a look at what you should start thinking about. You may not have to worry about *all* of these, but none of them can be done the night before you leave.

Living Arrangements

Most colleges assign freshman to specific dormitories. If your college offers you a choice of living arrangements, make your decision promptly and send in the necessary forms without delay. Many campuses have a housing shortage: The early bird gets the room.

Here's a story to curl your hair. Pete waited and waited and never sent in the rooming information requested by his college. The week before he left, he was notified of assignment to a "temporary double." He arrived to find himself sharing a small single room. Then Pete was moved into a double with a roommate who never took a shower. Pete hastily moved again— this time into a closet-sized single. Finally, four weeks later, he was assigned to a permanent double. Pete is eloquent on the subject of sending in your room request information early—the day it arrives in the mail.

Fee Deadlines

If you fail to meet financial deadlines, you may lose your place. Without exception, colleges make crystal clear what you have to pay and when you have to pay it. Part of your responsibility in accepting admission to college is meeting the institution's tuition and fee requirements on time.

Summer Jobs

Many students plan to work the summer after high school graduation to make money to help meet college expenses. A summer job won't fall into your lap the day after graduation, so start looking early. And plan ahead: If your college wants you on campus by late August, a job that runs through Labor Day is not for you. It's unrealistic to work right up to the day before you leave, so allow yourself a few days to get everything together.

Once your living and financial decisions have been made, you can take a breather—for a while. But you can't relax indefinitely.

Technical Tune-ups

Come September, you'll be reading more, taking more notes, and writing more papers than you've ever had to in your life. The time to polish up your skills is now, before you attend your first lecture.

Here are some things to consider:

Reading Skills
A slow reader may want to take a speed reading course or a reading skills course to improve reading comprehension. Your high school or local community college may offer such courses. If not, check a local library or bookstore for books to help you brush up on those skills independently.

Writing Skills
If you don't write as well as you would like, you may want to take a course to improve your writing skills as well. Check with your high school, the local commu-

nity college, or the college you're going to attend to find out what is offered.

Typing Skills

Are you a hunt-and-peck typist? The summer before you go to college is a perfect time to learn how to touch-type. You can get a book and teach yourself, or you can take a course. Most people find it easier with a teacher to direct and encourage them. Touch-typing is an enormous time-saver and a marketable skill, particularly when it comes to using a computer keyboard.

Computer Skills

If you've never used a computer, you may want to take a computer course that will introduce you to the basics of what computers can do and how to operate them. Your high school may offer summer programs in these subjects for a reasonable fee. Technical and vocational schools offer a variety of courses in this field. You can also check out nearby colleges or get a list of computer courses from your state education department.

The material your college sends you will probably include information about computer facilities and the kinds of hardware and software students find useful. If you have a question, call the college computer center. (For more information on computers in college, see "Academic Basics" in Chapter 3.)

Medical Matters

Doctors' Appointments

Many colleges require a form to prove you've had a recent physical check-up and are in good health. Don't wait until the last minute to make an appointment with your general practitioner, and to see your internist, allergist, gynecologist, opthalmologist, dermatologist, or dentist if necessary, because August is traditionally vacation month for doctors. And if you don't have information about birth control but would like to, consult your doctor or the local Planned Parenthood office. Keep in mind that most colleges have their own health services, with doctors and nurses on staff who can help you when you are sick, dispense medication, and provide a range of support and referral services, from birth control to specialized medical care.

If you wear glasses and have been dying to get contact lenses, make the change as soon as possible so that you can get comfortable with them by September. If you want to have another pair of glasses with jazzier frames, order them now. It's a good idea to take a spare pair with you, and to have a copy of your prescription just in case.

Getting in Shape
Conditioning isn't just for athletes. If you've been threatening to start an exercise program, or lose some serious weight, the summer before college is a fine time to start. You'll look and feel much better.

Health Insurance
Check into health insurance coverage. Many colleges offer inexpensive insurance plans, but you may be better off sticking with your parents' coverage. Compare the costs and benefits of the different policies in terms of deductibles and accident and illness coverage.

3

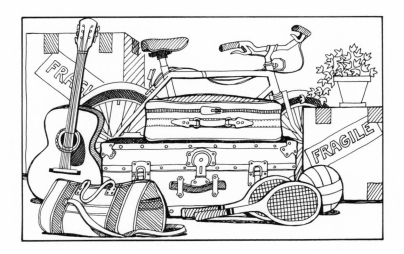

What Do I Need To Take?

You may feel there's a mountain of stuff you can't live without, and you don't know how to begin deciding what to take and what to leave behind. Mountains can be broken down into little hills. It helps to think in categories.

First of all, *clothes.*

Are you going to New Mexico, New York, or New Hampshire? The climate and location—urban, suburban, or rural—are big factors in deciding what kinds of clothes to take to college. Equally important, of course, is the campus style. Is it simple or sophisticated? What's your personal style?

Bear in mind that, in the words of a wise Stanford sophomore: life revolves around laundry. When asked what he wished he'd brought as a freshman, he said, "More underwear! And more socks. Especially if you're sort of a jock. Before you know it you're out of clean everything. Let's face it—the more you've got, the less often you have to do laundry. And I think doing laundry is the pits."

Clothing Basics

Here's a student-tested, unisex list of clothing suggestions that should prove useful.

- ☐ Underwear and socks—as many as you need
- ☐ Two pairs of denim jeans
- ☐ Four pairs of slacks (linen, corduroy, wool, flannel)
- ☐ A pair of khakis/army pants/overalls
- ☐ Five long-sleeved shirts (cotton, cotton/polyester, flannel, knit)

- ☐ Four turtlenecks
- ☐ Five sweaters (crewneck, V-neck, cardigan)
- ☐ Several pairs of shorts and T-shirts
- ☐ Pajamas or nightshirts
- ☐ A denim jacket
- ☐ A blazer or a tweed sports jacket
- ☐ A warm winter coat or down jacket
- ☐ A raincoat or slicker
- ☐ Waterproof boots and leather boots
- ☐ Sports shoes—depending on your game
- ☐ Dress shoes
- ☐ Two sets of sweatshirts and sweatpants
- ☐ A belt or two
- ☐ Gloves
- ☐ A warm scarf
- ☐ A hat

Leave Your Mark

Most denim jackets, raincoats, and gray sweatshirts look pretty much alike. If you leave one of yours at the library or the cafeteria and want to have a prayer of ever seeing it again, mark your name on the label in indelible ink or sew or iron on a name tape.

Once you get to school, you may find that certain clothes are "in" on your campus. For example, at Howard University, almost all the students who come from Africa wear dashikis, and so do some of the U.S. students. And one Princeton freshman noted that everyone she's met wears very sloppy clothes, but the sloppiness is carefully calculated.

Wise words came from a Loyola sophomore: "At first you keep looking around and thinking, 'Oh, what's she wearing?', but once classes start and you all get to know each other, you find out it's what they're really like that matters."

The checklists that follow will help you figure out just what you're going to need—and want—on campus.

Underwear, Legwear, and Sleepwear Checklist

Marilyn Monroe, when asked what she slept in, replied, "Chanel No. 5." You may want to choose a more tangible cover-up, especially if you will be living in a co-ed dorm. A lot of students say they like to sleep in sweats.

And, you've probably been warned about the embarrassment of being in an accident, taken to the hospital, and being discovered in less than pristine underwear, so be prepared.

Men	*Women*
_____ Boxer shorts	_____ Bras: athletic
_____ Jockey shorts	_____ Bras: other
_____ T-shirts	_____ Leotard
_____ Undershirts	_____ Panties
_____ Thermal underwear	_____ Slips
_____ Sweatshirts	_____ Sweatshirts
_____ Sweatpants	_____ Sweatpants
_____ Athletic socks	_____ Athletic socks
_____ Socks: other	_____ Socks: other
_____ Pajamas	_____ Kneesocks
_____ Robe	_____ Legwarmers
	_____ Tights
	_____ Pajamas
	_____ Nightie
	_____ Robe

Daywear Checklist

Daywear is just that—what you put on in the morning to get you through the day. The following items cover a wide range of locales and climates, so tailor the checklist to your needs. If you're going to the University of Hawaii, you know you can skip the wool vest and add some tropically inspired shorts and shirts!

Even young women who prefer pants will probably want to take a skirt or two along. Fashion is predictably unpredictable: Skirt lengths go up, skirt lengths come down, and these days you can wear whatever length suits you best.

Men	*Women*
_____ Shirts	_____ Shirts
_____ Shorts	_____ Shorts
_____ Scarves	_____ Scarves
_____ Sweaters	_____ Sweaters
_____ Vests	_____ Vests
_____ Jeans	_____ Jeans
_____ Slacks	_____ Slacks
_____ Overalls	_____ Overalls
_____ Belts	_____ Belts
_____ Sports jacket	_____ Blazer
_____ Blazer	_____ Suit
_____ Suit	_____ Jumpsuit
_____ Ties	_____ Dresses
	_____ Skirts
	_____ Purses
	_____ Jewelry

Formalwear Checklist

Even if evening clothes aren't likely to be a part of your college lifestyle, you might consider investing in at least one outfit—just in case.

Men

Some clothes—a tuxedo, for instance—are strictly for waiters in fancy restaurants and special occasions such as weddings and award dinners. Generally, men rent this sort of thing. But if you're invited to lots of black-tie events—or you play in an orchestra, for example—you should think about buying because it's cheaper in the long run.

_____ Tuxedo
_____ White tie and tails
_____ Dinner jacket
_____ Dark suit

Women

When you're invited to a formal dance, it helps to know that you have a gorgeous dress and the right accessories in your closet.

_____ Evening dress
_____ Long skirt
_____ Dressy top
_____ Dress shoes
_____ Evening bag

Outerwear Checklist

Even if you're going south, there will probably be days when you'll need rain gear or a light jacket.

_____ Coat
_____ Jacket
_____ Down jacket
_____ Down vest
_____ Denim jacket
_____ Poncho
_____ Raincoat or slicker
_____ Windbreaker
_____ Earmuffs
_____ Hat
_____ Scarf
_____ Gloves
_____ Mittens
_____ Umbrella

Carryalls

Be sure you have one of the following items to carry around the books, papers, calculator, pens, pencils, emergency snack, and any other odds and ends you'll need in the course of a busy day.

_____ Backpack
_____ Bookbag
_____ Briefcase
_____ Purse

Shoes and Boots Checklist

Shoes

Some people live in the same pair of running shoes day in and day out. Others insist on different shoes for every occasion and activity. Since most people fall somewhere between those extremes, the following list is easy to tailor to your individual needs.

_____ Clogs

_____ Flats

_____ Heels

_____ Loafers

_____ Topsiders or moccasins

_____ Oxfords

_____ Sneakers

_____ Sandals

_____ Slippers

_____ Thongs

Boots

"I brought six pairs of heels to Cornell," said Louisa, "but Ithaca's cold and hilly and everything is so spread out that I live in hiking boots."

Depending on where you're going and whether you're an outdoor or an indoor person, here's some footgear to consider:

_____ Ankle

_____ Hiking

_____ Leather

_____ Ski

_____ Snow

_____ Waterproof

_____ Western

_____ Work

Sports Gear Checklist

In this era of specialization, there's specific gear for every activity. Use this list to check off your needs.

Activity	Clothing	Footwear	Equipment
Aerobics	——	——	——
Baseball	——	——	——
Basketball	——	——	——
Beach	——	——	——
Biking	——	——	——
Dance	——	——	——
Field hockey	——	——	——
Football	——	——	——
Golf	——	——	——
Hiking	——	——	——
Hockey	——	——	——
Lacrosse	——	——	——
Rugby	——	——	——
Scuba	——	——	——
Skating	——	——	——
Skiing	——	——	——
Snorkeling	——	——	——
Soccer	——	——	——
Squash	——	——	——
Swimming	——	——	——
Tennis	——	——	——
——	——	——	——
——	——	——	——

Personal Necessities

"You'll be totally amazed at what it costs to buy shampoo, deodorant, toothpaste, and shaving cream," said Gerry as he packed up to go back to college in New York City. "What I do, the night before I take off, is raid the bathroom cabinet and stock up."

It's probably a good idea to check with your parents before you do this. But unless you've been buying these items regularly, you'll find they take a surprising chunk out of your budget.

Once you're in the dorm, unless you find yourself living in unexpected luxury with an adjoining bathroom of your own, you're going to have to carry many of these items back and forth from the bathroom down the hall. At some schools students use small plastic pails. Or you can take a toilet kit or a waterproof case.

The following list of personal items covers what students typically take along. Tailor it to your needs.

Personal Necessities Checklist

Hair

_____ Barrettes and hairbands
_____ Brush
_____ Comb
_____ Curling iron
_____ Hairdryer
_____ Shampoo
_____ Conditioner

Health

_____ Cold and allergy medication
_____ Aspirin
_____ Band-Aids
_____ Cough medicine
_____ Laxative
_____ Vitamins

Teeth and mouth

_____ Dental floss
_____ Mouthwash
_____ Toothbrush
_____ Toothpaste

Body and face

_____ Cosmetics
_____ Deodorant
_____ Nail polish
_____ Nail polish remover
_____ Perfume
_____ Shaving cream
_____ Shaving brush
_____ Razor
_____ Face soap
_____ Body soap
_____ Soap dish
_____ Talc

Eyes

_____ Contact lens cleaning material

Other

_____ Tissues
_____ Cotton balls
_____ Tampons or pads
_____ Laundry bag
_____ Safety pins
_____ Sewing kit
_____ Travel alarm

Room Essentials

Freshmen living on campus are usually assigned to freshman dorms. You may dream of a single or a comfortable double; however, colleges are grappling with housing shortages and we've heard many a story about three people in a 12-by-12-foot room designed for two, and even five squeezed into a room intended for three.

Be prepared to be flexible. Think small. Think organized. Think practical. Think about *not* bringing eleven stuffed animals and all your posters.

Find out what your roommates are bringing. Four students in the same living space rarely require four stereos. On the other hand, your own Walkman lets you select the music and decibel level you prefer without disturbing anyone.

Find out what the college provides, but be prepared for unwelcome surprises. A New Jersey freshman who'd been told there would be a desk in her room was shaken to find no desk and no space for one. You may even find yourself perched on the top of a bunk bed with your closet in the room next door.

You'll manage, although your parents may get slightly hysterical. Try to distract them while you think of the stories you'll be able to tell about how you survived freshman year.

You'll want to make your room feel more like home, but before you start nailing two-by-fours or hammering picture hooks into the walls, check with your resident adviser or the housing office to make sure you're not breaking any rules.

Many students feel that a telephone is a necessity. Not all colleges agree, so before you do anything about a phone, check to find out your school's regulations. If you're allowed to have a phone, the college can provide information about how to arrange for installation. (See "Where the Money Goes" in Chapter Four for more information on phones.)

Some students like having a refrigerator handy. Again, not all colleges allow them, so inquire before you make any definite arrangements. "My two roommates and I decided to get a fridge because we never get up for breakfast and we keep milk and yogurt and fruit in it," said Martha of the University of Miami. "I also kept my underwear in there when it was really hot!" If your college permits refrigerators in the dorm but you're not sure whether you really need one, rent one for a month. If you decide to keep it for the year, it may pay to buy. Many students manage without a refrigerator. Some dorms have small snack rooms with vending machines and a refrigerator.

Of course you'll need linens and towels. Take at least four towels. Bigger is better. If you're a swimmer or a compulsive bather, take more. Also, you'll want something to wake you up in the morning. An alarm clock or clock radio with batteries is a good idea if you don't have a lot of outlets in your room.

Lighting will be important. Do you need a desk lamp? A floor lamp? A light by the bed? If you read in bed at night, a clip-on book light won't keep your roommate awake.

Will you need a desk chair? If you have room, a foam chair that flips open and turns into a bed is great to have when a friend comes to visit.

The dustballs under your bed may only catch your eye the day before your parents come to visit. Or you may discover that you are fanatical about keeping your room tidy. You should find out from the custodian if you can borrow brooms, dustpans, or a vacuum. You probably have some clothes that will need ironing. We recommend an iron with an automatic shut-off so you don't burn the dorm down. If your room doesn't have a decent mirror, buy an inexpensive one locally. Packing a mirror is not worth it.

The room items checklist suggests the range of stuff you can consider for your room. If in doubt, leave it out. Or, to contradict a well-known slogan, *do* leave home without it. You can always bring it later or buy it.

Room Organizers

Once you've got all your stuff in your room, what are you going to do with it? Below are useful items to help you keep your belongings in order. Again—you can buy these once you get to college.

- ☐ Multiple shirt, skirt, and trouser hangers
- ☐ Regular hangers—you will find few if any in the closet
- ☐ Under-the-bed storage boxes—two or three will fit under your bed
- ☐ Hanging sweater bags—not only for sweaters, these function as additional shelves
- ☐ Folding shoe rack
- ☐ Plastic milk crates—these stack and provide extra storage
- ☐ A wastebasket
- ☐ A bulletin board

Cornell University's freshman booklet advises: "In an effort to preserve your teeth, it would be wise to bring a bottle opener, although door latches are usable as such. Of course, if you prefer the more alcoholic bubbly drink, a corkscrew might help."

- ☐ Bottle opener and corkscrew

Room Items Checklist

Telephone
Bring one? _____
For installation, call: _____
Your phone number: _____
Answering machine? _____

Refrigerator
Rent or buy? _____

Linens
Sheets (two sets) _____
Pillowcases _____
Pillows _____
Mattress pad/cover _____
Comforter or quilt _____
Blanket(s) _____
Bedspread _____
Air mattress/futon _____

Towels and washcloths _____

Alarm clock or clock radio _____

Lighting
Desk lamp _____
Floor lamp _____
Bed light _____
Clip-on book light _____

Seating
Desk chair _____
Foam chair _____

Cleaning equipment _____

Iron _____

Academic Basics

Remember the course catalog? You may not have looked at it in a while, but that array of educational offerings is the reason you're going to college.

> Perhaps the most valuable result of all education is the ability to make yourself do the thing you have to do, when it ought to be done, whether you like it or not; it is the first lesson that ought to be learned.
> —T. H. Huxley, biologist and author, 1825–1895

The first order of business at college is learning and the first place to begin is with your books. Any reference book you need can be found in your college library. However, there are some relatively inexpensive ones that are helpful to have on your desk. Here are some recommendations from teachers and students. You may not need every one of these books, but it's great to have ready access to them.

Reference Books

Webster's Ninth New Collegiate Dictionary—the most recent edition, or another standard unabridged dictionary. Undersized paperback dictionaries won't last for four years.

A *foreign-language dictionary* for your language studies. A language teacher can recommend one.

Concise Columbia Encyclopedia. This is the portable

version of *The New Columbia Encyclopedia,* published by Columbia University Press.

Roget's International Thesaurus, a source of synonyms, antonyms, and related words, published by Harper and Row.

The World Almanac or another comparable almanac.

The Elements of Style by William Strunk, Jr., and E. B. White, the classic writing manual, published by Macmillan.

An inexpensive paperbound atlas such as *The Rand-McNally Contemporary World Atlas.*

A Bible, including both Old and New Testaments. Even if you are not religious, it is a valuable reference tool.

The University of Chicago Press publishes a *Manual for Writers of Term Papers, Theses and Dissertations* by Kate L. Turabian, which is very widely used. However, your college may publish its own manual on researching and writing term papers. Check to see what your college recommends before buying a writing manual.

Finding Facts Fast: How to Find Out What You Want and Need to Know, by Alden Todd, is designed to help students learn the fastest and most thorough research techniques. It is published by Ten Speed Press.

The New York Times Guide to Reference Materials is recommended as a useful guide to reference books. It also includes information on using a library, writing a paper, and methods of research. It is published by Times Books in cloth; New American Library in paper.

Tools Checklist

If you were a carpenter, you would bring your hammer
to work. As a student, you work with different kinds of
tools. Check off what you need.

- ☐ A calculator—preferably a solar-powered model so
  you never have to worry about buying batteries.
- ☐ A pencil sharpener
- ☐ A stapler
- ☐ Paper clips
- ☐ Pens and pencils and "hi-liters"
- ☐ A pair of scissors
- ☐ A ruler
- ☐ A typewriter and ribbons. If you're acquiring a new
  typewriter, consider getting one with memory.
- ☐ A clipboard
- ☐ An erasable message board
- ☐ A roll of cellophane tape and dispenser

A special note on computers: If you already have a
computer, check with the college to find out whether
you should take it along. Not all dorms are set up for
computer use and some colleges require a specific type
of computer.

If you don't have a computer and are thinking of
buying one, wait until you get to school. From the
standpoint of price and compatibility, you'll probably
be better off.

More and more schools are requiring computers
and offer discounted prices. To give just one example,
in academic year 1987–88, Drexel Institute in Philadel-
phia *required* entering freshmen to purchase, for
$1,390, a package including a computer microproces-

sor, a video display monitor, a keyboard and mouse, a megabyte of memory and an 800k double-sided drive, plus six software packages. The purchase could be financed over the four-year college period.

This package did not include a printer. If you decide to buy one, you can print out drafts of your work as you go along, and you won't have to worry about access. On the other hand, a printer is expensive, takes up space, and is noisy. Many students use on-campus printers.

Personal Stuff

Only *you* know what makes you feel at home. Whatever it is—within reason—take it. Maybe you want to put up photos of your family and friends, or perhaps you'd like to have some favorite books with you. Students we've talked to have brought:

- [ ] A boom box—containing a radio, a cassette recorder, and a compact disc player. Or you may prefer a separate radio, portable cassette recorder, and stereo with a turntable.
- [ ] Stationery—for writing to friends.
- [ ] A popcorn popper—if allowed.
- [ ] A pair of binoculars—for dedicated bird-watchers or football fans.
- [ ] A camera—an inexpensive, automatic one to record those bright college days for posterity.
- [ ] A plant—needs water, light, and occasional feeding.
- [ ] A guitar, a recorder, a flute, a kazoo—or any other portable musical instrument that you enjoy playing.

☐ Posters—if you can't bear to be parted from Bruce Springsteen or your SANE poster. But remember, your college bookstore will have a great selection.

One freshman carefully transported an aquarium and seven fish. One angel fish, sad to say, died in transit. The other six are reported to be doing well in the second half of their freshman year. But see "What Not to Take," later in this chapter, for some disadvantages to taking pets to college.

Another freshman, thanks to her film producer father, arrived with a life-sized cardboard figure of Warren Beatty. He immediately felt quite at home in the six-woman suite!

Great Gifts to Ask For

One of the nice things about graduating from high school and going to college is that people have an urge to give you presents.

When family and friends ask what you would like, be prepared to tell them. You might just get it!

Look over the lists of things you're planning to buy: Gift-givers will be relieved if you tell them that you really *need* a calculator, an iron, or a pair of fur-lined gloves. Be truthful—if you don't yearn for a designer pen and pencil set, say so, and ask for the travel alarm you really want.

Maybe your aunt will buy you the Spanish-English dictionary you need. Your sister can get you a supply of blank audio tapes. Your uncle, whose alma mater you're going to, might be delighted to give you a foam chairbed, especially since he wants his son, who's going into his senior year, to visit you. Duffels, book bags, and other pieces of luggage make excellent presents.

How about a mug or two for late-night hot chocolate? Or a key ring for your new room keys? Or a multiple picture frame? If you know that your tennis racket is beyond help or needs restringing, perhaps your best friend's parents will take care of that instead of buying the hand-tooled, red leather desk set you'd be too embarrassed to use. And if you find a denim jacket that you absolutely must have and it's wildly expensive, there may be grandparents who would be happy to get it for you.

The point is that you are going to be asked what you'd like and you may as well be prepared. Know what you need and are permitted to bring with you. Do find out from the dorm counselor or the housing office if you are allowed to use electrical appliances in your room before you acquire a hotplate, a toaster oven, or a coffeemaker.

Though we haven't included these in any of our lists, games—such as backgammon, chess, Monopoly, and Trivial Pursuit—are great icebreakers. For the sports lover, a Nerf basketball set is a great way to vent some pent-up energy without breaking up the furniture.

Sometimes a present brings unexpected benefits with it. "My godparents gave me a popcorn popper, complete with a large jar of gourmet popcorn," said Gretchen. "My very first night at Oberlin, I made a batch and everyone on my corridor came in and we sat around and talked until two."

What Not to Take

Pets

Most colleges prohibit pets. You may love your hamster, but he probably doesn't need a college education. Neither does your parakeet, which is why most para-

keets stay home. Even the fish that may adjust success-
fully to dorm life are not ideal roommates: What would
you do with them over spring break? What if there's a
power failure and the oxygen pump in the fish tank
goes off? How is a fish tank going to fit into your pint-
sized room, anyway?

Valuables

You should also leave behind valuables like fine jew-
elry, an expensive watch, elaborate camera equipment,
or any precious memento you'd hate to lose. It isn't
pleasant to think that there are thieves in the college
community; however, things do get taken and one way
to protect yourself is to be cautious about what you
leave in your room.

Cash

You'll need money, of course, but you are better off
with traveler's checks or a checking account, or a
credit card than a lot of loose cash. Money gets a whole
chapter to itself (Chapter 4).

Luggage Logic

Suitcases, boxes, duffel bags, backpacks, shopping bags,
trunks, large plastic bags, shoe boxes—what are you going to put your stuff in?

Start by analyzing your luggage needs. Will you be
traveling frequently? Will you be taking long or short
trips? Will you be traveling by plane, bus, train, or car?

If you're flying, you have to consider weight and
size restrictions as well as the number of bags you can
take. Currently, you can check two pieces of baggage

per passenger, 70 pounds maximum weight per piece. Carry-on luggage may not exceed 40 pounds.

Check with the airline or your travel agent for specific baggage information, but remember that excess baggage costs are expensive. It's always easier, quicker, and safer to deal with carry-on luggage rather than baggage that has to be checked through.

Similarly, buses and trains often have space limitations. And, of course, not all car trunks are created equal.

Luggage comes in a wide variety of shapes, sizes, and materials. Hard cases are usually heavier than soft-sided cases but offer separate compartments for more organized packing and greater protection for what's inside. Soft luggage offers packing flexibility because you can stuff more things in.

Cheap luggage is never a bargain. It's worth investing in well-made bags that will last you through your four years of college and beyond. Nylon luggage is very sturdy and sometimes lined for additional strength. Vinyl luggage is washable and very durable, and cotton canvas, which is lightweight, may be vinyl-lined. Hard-sided baggage is usually made of molded materials.

You can find a style of bag to suit your needs. Among the most useful are garment bags, large- and medium-sized suitcases, duffels, totes, and lightweight carry-ons. Some students pack trunks that are later used as tables and for storage.

When shopping for luggage, look for these features:

- Nesting luggage—where one piece fits inside the other for easy storage
- Wheels—these are especially useful on large suitcases
- Plastic interior pockets—for separating damp or dirty clothing

- Packing straps—to keep things in place and prevent wrinkling
- Cushioned handles and shoulder straps—make carrying more comfortable
- Exterior pockets on totes and carry-ons—for tickets and reading material
- Pockets on garment bags—for toiletries, underwear, and shoes
- Locking hanger fixtures—which hold standard hangers in place
- Internal and external baggage tags—to identify your luggage if it goes astray.

Preparing to Pack

Whether you are sending most of your things ahead or taking them with you, you're going to need some sturdy cardboard boxes. Recommended sources are local liquor stores or supermarkets.

Packing Supplies Checklist

	Do I need?	*Do I have?*	*How many?*
Boxes			
Suitcases			
Trunks			
Duffel bags			
Backpack			
Garment bags			
Other			

You'll probably take most of your stuff with you if you are driving to school. If you don't drive, you'll have to ship most of it ahead and travel with a couple of suitcases, a duffel bag, or a backpack.

The Post Office advises you to pack properly and ship in plenty of time. Whatever you send must be taken over to the post office or United Parcel Service. It's a good idea to find out what restrictions your mailing service puts on packages—on the size, packing materials used, etc. Use sturdy cartons; allow room inside for cushioning material, keeping fragile items away from the sides and corners. Seal all seams with strong packing tape. String or masking or cellophane tape aren't strong enough. Reinforced packing tape is easier to use and sturdier. Be sure the mailing label and return label are as accurate as you can make them. For added protection, put a duplicate label inside the carton.

Depending on how far you're sending your stuff, UPS usually guarantees delivery within six days. There are speedier but more expensive services such as Express Mail, Federal Express, UPS Next or Second Day Air, or Purolator. Planning ahead and mailing early can save you money.

Packing Tips

What about the stuff you take with you?

- Pack one case with items you'll need on the first day so you have a clean shirt and can wash your hair without unpacking everything.
- Carry toiletries in leakproof plastic bags.
- Rolling your clothes is an easy way to pack casual items like pants, pajamas, and underwear.

- Tissue paper layered between garments helps avoid wrinkling.
- Pack shoes in plastic bags and tuck them into the bottom corners of your luggage. Stuff socks into shoes.
- Keep your tickets, travel documents, traveler's checks, driver's license, hotel and car rental confirmations, and trunk keys with you—don't pack any of these away in checked baggage.
- Don't throw away any of the boxes from the presents people give you. If you're packing up a computer or stereo, it's a good idea to keep it in its original packing carton.

Money Matters

It may be that you're a financial wizard, have your own stockbroker, follow the market, and understand that selling short has nothing to do with height. Or perhaps you're an entrepreneur who sells elaborate gingerbread houses at holiday time, or makes videos of children's parties. Perhaps you know about bank accounts, cash flow, and balancing your budget. For many students, however, who only babysit occasionally or just work over the summer, budgeting their meager earnings is an alien and depressing concept. Others don't bother to budget because they know they don't have to.

Mitch, now a Villanova senior, worked in high school and banked his earnings. "At college," he said, "I opened a checking account to cover my expenses and my parents sent me a lump sum each semester to take care of books and clothing. They paid the tuition. I've never had a budget—I don't even note the checks I write. It's a hassle to keep track. It's a decision you make, though it's a risk. I consider it a trade-off."

While it may be appealing to think of floating through college spending money at will, most students have to learn to budget their day-to-day living expenses over extended periods of time. Different families work out different systems to match their resources and their attitudes toward money. How you organize your finances is something you should talk about with your parents.

There is an extensive range of awards and scholarships available to meet college expenses. If it's not too late, check out the thousands of special scholarships— for athletes; for people whose parents work for certain companies; for students of Czechoslovakian or Finnish ancestry; for residents of specific communities; for inner-city students; and for 4-H-ers. If you didn't apply this year, you may be able to qualify next year.

Before you leave home, be clear about who is going to pay for what. It's to your advantage, after all, to know that you'll have a certain amount of money each month, and that if you blow November's money on a CD player you'll be too broke to buy presents in December.

Where the Money Goes

It's no mystery where the money goes. The biggest chunks go to pay for tuition and room and board, and you already have a pretty good idea of what these are going to cost you.

But how are you going to estimate all other expenses that come weekly, monthly, or at the beginning or end of each semester? You will find some realistic projections in the financial advice and information your college sends you. Below are some ballpark figures for your most common expenses.

Deciding on a Meal Plan

Usually, for about $2,000, students get 19 meals a week—that's three meals a day from Monday through Friday and two meals a day on weekends. Most colleges also offer a range of plans that cover fewer meals, and these are priced accordingly. Freshmen are usually required to sign up for one of these meal plans in order to encourage them to eat most of their meals on campus. Most freshmen find that the dining hall is one of the easiest places to meet and talk with other students.

When you sign up for a meal plan, you will be able to indicate special food requirements such as kosher, diabetic, or vegetarian meals.

Textbooks

Depending on the courses you take, you're going to need about $200 a semester for textbooks. Try to get to the bookstores early because they get unbelievably crowded. If you procrastinate, a book might be out of stock and it can be weeks before new books arrive.

Buying used books is one way of keeping costs down. You can sometimes buy used books at a discount of 25 percent or more and sell them after the course for about half of what you paid. But a book isn't a bargain if the previous owner has made so many notes on the pages that it's impossible to use. Examine carefully before you buy.

Save your receipts: If you decide to drop a course after the first few classes, you can usually return the books for a full refund if you haven't written in them.

Supplies

Just like every other September when you started a new school year, you're going to lay in a supply of notebooks, folders, pens, and pencils. You'll probably want either a separate notebook or a separate section of a large looseleaf binder for each course. You can figure out how much five individual notebooks or a big, all-purpose one will cost you and add on the amounts for whatever else you need. You will probably spend between $35 and $70 on supplies.

Campus Transportation

Think twice before you bring a car to college in your freshman year. Many schools discourage cars on campus because parking is a problem: They may also require an automobile registration fee. Usually, undergraduates don't have parking privileges unless there are special circumstances. You may find yourself paying to park your car—or paying for the tickets and towing costs when you park it illegally. What's more, insurance, gas, and maintenance—costs your parents may have taken care of for years—are going to put a large dent in your budget.

Some colleges provide free shuttle buses, particularly when the campus is spread out over a large area. Or you can use public transportation to get around campus and into town. Depending on how hilly and chilly your campus is, you may decide to bring your bike. Many college campuses are small enough and close enough to town to get around by foot.

Unless you do bring a car or are an inveterate taxi-taker, your campus transportation costs should be minimal—probably no more than $5 a week.

The Phone Question

Under most circumstances it's cheaper to buy a phone than to rent from the phone company. If your college allows phones and you have your own at home, bring it with you: Many rooms already have jacks, so you can just plug it in once you've arranged for service.

Check the installation costs and the monthly rates. Depending on the phone company, you may have to leave a deposit when you start service. There may also be a start-up fee. Local and long distance rates vary according to the company you choose and the kind of service you select. For example, if you and your roommates want "Call Waiting," you will have to pay a little extra for it.

"The only thing my roommate and I ever had a fight about was the phone bill," said Anna Jane. "The phone was in my name, so I was responsible. When the bill came in and we tried to divide up the long distance charges, we could never remember who called Ohio and who spent thirty-five minutes on the phone to Boston. I got stuck more than once."

If you don't share a phone, you can avoid a lot of problems. Otherwise, keep a pad by the phone for every caller to write down the date and number of long distance calls.

Long distance rates may not matter to you unless your girlfriend goes to school in Louisiana and you're at the University of Colorado and your parents have retired to Hawaii. Check into this . . . or, if nobody protests, call collect!

The key question is: How much are you going to use the telephone? Some young people have a phone permanently glued to one ear. They must have a lengthy phone fix each day or they develop alarming withdrawal symptoms. Take a look at your parents' recent phone bills and try to estimate what percentage you were responsible for. Did you realize that you spent 47 minutes on the phone to your sister at Berkeley?

It may be hard to work out how much you're going to use the phone during your first few months at college, but it's probably going to be a lot more than you think. It would be a good idea to estimate on the high

side—somewhere between $35 and $100—and your
first phone bill won't be as much of a shock.

Laundry

Your clothes are going to get dirty and you're going to
have to get them clean. Most dorms have washers and
dryers. Instructions for how to operate them are clearly
printed—usually inside the lid of the washer, and next
to the coin box of the dryer. Sometimes they are posted
on the laundry room wall as well. Or, if you're not sure
what to do, ask another student with a basket full of
dirty laundry if you can watch how he does it.

If you haven't communicated with machines like
this before, consider the cautionary experience of one
young man at a highly selective private college. After
two weeks at school, he picked his dirty clothes off the
floor and took them down to the laundry room in the
basement of his dorm. He carefully dumped them into
the machine, added the requisite amount of powdered
detergent, and deposited two quarters as instructed.
When he saw his laundry swirling behind the little
round window, he went back upstairs.

An hour later, he returned. The machine had
stopped. He opened the door. The clothing was very
warm. It was speckled with grains of detergent. To his
surprise, nothing was any cleaner. With an I.Q. of 158,
he was bewildered. Then a helpful sophomore came to
his rescue: "You put your stuff in the dryer," she said.
She was kind enough not to laugh.

Cleaning your clothes will mean feeding the washer
and dryer about once a week. If you're doing sheets and
towels, that's another load. A washer usually takes a
couple of quarters, and most dryers run for ten minutes
on a dime. You can wash some items—like fragile un-

dies and sweaters—by hand. Dry cleaning is more expensive, so try to keep it to a minimum. If you follow the tips above, somewhere around $10 a month should take care of your laundry needs.

Recreation

You're on your own here. If you're going to purchase a season ticket to all home football games, you'll know what this is going to add up to.

If you're a movie buff, tickets will cost you. Often colleges have film societies offering movies at bargain prices. And a lot of college towns have revival or art film houses catering to the college crowd.

On your campus you may also find theater, concerts, dances, poetry readings, visiting lecturers, and more.

One member of the Student Union board of a large Midwestern university estimated that he spent approximately $10 a week on entertainment, not counting eating out. "There is always an amazing amount going on here," he said, "and you can always find something cheap to do."

How about eating out? Partying? Taking trips? The best things in life are free, they say, but these are not.

Peter goes to a small college in New England. He finds he spends his money traveling into Boston to visit friends and go to museums and concerts. "The main weekend activity was partying at the frat houses," he said. "That's fun sometimes, but I need to get away." He estimated that he spent at least $25 to $40 a week on entertainment, except during exams.

Libby, from Colorado, goes to Columbia University in New York City. "I could spend a fortune," she noted. "There is so much going on—ski trips to the

Berkshires, chamber music, vintage films I've never seen, the whole of Manhattan! I hate to miss out, but it's much more expensive than I imagined." Libby takes advantage of student discounts and lower-priced preview tickets, but she knows she could easily spend over $200 a month on entertainment.

Travel

How much will it cost to get home?

Think this through. Are we talking about cross-country airfare, bus tickets, train fare, or paying for half the gas?

Since you probably know when you'll be traveling, you may be able to take advantage of bargain fares by booking well in advance. However, students generally travel at holiday times when lots of other people are traveling, too, so book early to make sure you get a seat even though there may not be a reduced rate available. (See "Four Weeks Before You Leave" in Chapter 5 for more on travel arrangements.)

Estimated Travel Costs

To _____ When _____ Cost _____

To _____ When _____ Cost _____

To _____ When _____ Cost _____

To _____ When _____ Cost _____

To _____ When _____ Cost _____

To _____ When _____ Cost _____

Total $ _____

Most students come home at the end of each semester, for Thanksgiving, Christmas, spring break, and for the summer. Estimate what a round-trip costs and how many times you're going to make the trip.

Miscellaneous

Expect some unexpected expenses. What if you lose a contact lens and have to replace it? What if your sneakers disappear from the gym? What if you lose your Spanish text?

Sooner or later, you're going to need a haircut. What if you want to buy somebody a present? What if Billy Joel appears in concert and you can actually get a ticket? What if it's too hot to sleep in your room without a fan?

It's a good idea to have a hundred dollars or so put aside for emergencies.

Budget Estimate	
	One Semester
Textbooks	_____
Supplies	_____
Campus transportation	_____
Telephone	_____
Laundry	_____
Recreation	_____
Travel	_____
Miscellaneous	_____
Estimated Total	_____

Sense and Dollars

You and your parents have to agree on a money management arrangement that reflects how much money is available and how responsibly you can handle it. Mitch, as we saw, was able to "go with the flow" because his parents accepted and could afford his relaxed attitude toward spending. Many other parents, regardless of their income level, would not recommend that approach.

Carole and her parents agreed that she would be responsible for providing $1,000 toward her college expenses each year. She could earn it any time—at a summer job or during the year on campus. Her parents took care of her other expenses.

"I liked this arrangement because I thought it was fair and I felt as though I was contributing," said Carole. "The summer between freshman and sophomore year, for instance, I made over a thousand dollars waiting on tables on Cape Cod. Then when I had a very heavy workload in the fall semester I didn't have to worry about earning money."

Enrique's mother deposits a fixed, agreed-upon amount into their joint checking account every two weeks. He takes his everyday living expenses from this account. When he realized that he was always running out of money, he got a job for five hours a week returning books to the stacks of the law library.

"My mom offered to give me more money, but I knew she really couldn't afford it," he said. "Besides, the library is right near my dorm and five hours a week is no big deal."

Lin receives a lump sum for tuition, plus a monthly check from her parents that goes into her college checking account. Out of this monthly payment she takes care of room and board and all her living expenses. She is expected to keep a detailed budget.

"My folks and I agreed before I left that I would learn how to manage my money at college. When I go home my father and I go over my budget and make adjustments if we need to. I hate the idea of having to call my parents for money, and I think this system has made me a more independent person. I'll tell you one thing: It certainly makes you think twice before you go and get your hair cut."

On her first day walking around her college town, Penny saw the stereo speakers of her dreams. She hesitated because they were expensive.

Her mother said, "It's your budget and your decision. You're in charge of your money now."

Penny bought the equipment. At the end of the term, she called home and asked her mom to send her a check. "I'm so broke," she said, "that I don't even have enough money to buy shampoo."

"Well, dear," said her mother wryly, "you can always wash your hair with your speakers."

Checking Accounts

It's easier to cash checks and pay by check at local stores if your bank account is in your college community rather than out of town. Banks vary in the services they offer: Some provide free checking if you keep a minimum balance in your checking account or in a savings account; some may give interest on checking accounts. It may pay you to open a savings account.

Banks today are competitive, so shop around for the best deal, bearing in mind that location is very important. You don't want to have to take a bus or bicycle over to the next town every time you need some cash.

You'll probably want to acquire a cash card from your bank so that you can withdraw money at any time. Most banks now have automatic cash machines.

Credit Cards

Credit cards like Mastercard or Visa are convenient but seductive. They are particularly useful if you're going to have major expenses like airline tickets. They are particularly dangerous if you carry them around and whip them out to pay for lots of small items without realizing how the charges—and the substantial interest rates—are adding up.

You may find it helps to use a charge card such as American Express, which does not extend credit, and requires complete payment every month. Knowing you must pay the entire amount you have spent every month may be just the incentive you need not to spend too much!

One parent said, "After we got Donald's Visa bill for December, we told him not to use it except for major purchases, which had to be cleared with us first."

If your college has a co-op, you can get a charge card and may benefit from co-op refund policies at the end of the year. For example, the Harvard Co-op is run as a nonprofit company. When you pay for your purchases with a Co-op card, a record is kept. At the end of the school year, you receive a rebate of approximately 10 percent.

Tracking Your Expenses

It's a good idea to keep track of what you spend your money on because you are in a new situation and money will trickle through your fingers and evaporate if you're not careful.

Louisa and Carole admitted that they were a little over-enthusiastic when it came to decorating their room. "We saw this brass hatstand in an antique shop that we simply had to have, and then the owner said he'd throw in the rug and the two wicker chairs for a couple of hundred more. Only when we got home did we realize how much we'd spent!" Carole said that she didn't want to tell her parents she needed money, "so I was really strapped for cash for the next two months."

It's not hard to create and label a bunch of budget columns. Like the diet you start on Monday and abandon on Thursday, it's sticking to it that's tough. However, you'll feel better—and you'll have an answer for your parents—if you know what you're spending your money on. You don't have to be fanatical about accounting for every penny, but you should note checks as you write them and write down everyday expenses.

A word of warning: Shakespeare knew what he was talking about when he wrote, "Neither a borrower nor a lender be." More people get stung than you would think. It's very hard to say no to a good friend who says, "I'm really broke; can you lend me some money?" It's hard to be clear about when and how you expect to be repaid, and it's uncomfortable when you have to remind someone to pay you back.

Some people are very irresponsible when it comes

to money, and some of your friends may fall into this category. You have to make the decision for yourself, but you should be aware that many friendships come to grief when money is involved.

In the chart below, you can see how David kept track of one week's expenses, dividing his expenses into two categories, Personal and Educational.

Joe, whose father is an accountant, wanted Joe to break down his expenses into detailed categories that included tuition, room and board; health and medical; books; supplies; telephone; laundry; transportation; recreation; travel; and other. If you want to keep track of your expenses, the forms that follow should meet your needs.

David's Budget

Week of 9/3–9/9

Date	Item	Personal	Educational	Total
9/3	math text		$24.95	$24.95
9/3	psych text		$19.95	19.95
9/3	desk lamp	$12.50		12.50
9/3	pizza	$7.00		7.00
9/4	supplies		$6.19	6.19
9/4	ice cream	$1.25		1.25
9/7	laundry	$2.50		2.50
9/7	movie	$4.75		4.75
9/8	drugstore	$8.50		8.50
9/8	English texts		$35.00	35.00
9/8	sweatshirt	$13.95		13.95
9/9	dinner	$11.00		11.00
			Weekly Total	$147.54

Expenses Record (Simple System)

Date	Item	Personal	Educational	Total

Expenses Record (Simple System)

Date	Item	Personal	Educational	Total

Expenses Record (Detailed Version)

Date	Item	Total	Tuition, room & board	Health/ Medical	Books & supplies	Phone, laundry, transp.	Recreation & travel	Other	Notes

Expenses Record (Detailed Version)

Date	Item	Total	Tuition, room & board	Health/ Medical	Books & supplies	Phone, laundry, transp.	Recreation & travel	Other	Notes

5

College Countdown

Based on our own experience and advice from many of the students we have talked to, we've devised one way to pace your precollege preparations. But you know what you're like, how you work best, and what makes you crazy. The following timetable gets everything done: Adjust it to suit your style.

Four Weeks Before You Leave

People to Contact

Roommate(s)
You'll probably receive the name(s), address(es), and phone number(s) of your roommate(s) sometime during the summer. If you get in touch before you start packing, you can find out who's bringing what and avoid duplication. You may also get some good ideas about things to take and things to leave behind. Food for thought: Everyone we talked with said, "Don't bring a TV set freshman year."

Dorm Counselors
You may get a letter from your dorm counselor, the upperclassperson in charge of your living unit. Don't be shy about calling to ask whether you can bring your aquarium, if every room has a bookcase, or whatever you want to know about the dorm situation. Dorm counselors were freshmen not very long ago, so they understand your concerns and can help you get a sense of what to expect.

Dorm Counselor's Name _____

Phone _____

Roommate(s)

Roommate's name _____

Address _____

_____ Phone _____

Roommate's name _____

Address _____

_____ Phone _____

Roommate's name _____

Address _____

_____ Phone _____

Roommate's name _____

Address _____

_____ Phone _____

What My Roommate(s) Said They'd Bring

_____

_____

_____

_____

_____

What I Said I'd Bring

_____

_____

_____

_____

You and Your Gear

The challenge is to move you and your stuff out of your house and into your dorm room with minimal wear and tear.

Start with Yourself
If you're flying or taking a bus or train to college, make sure you reserve space well ahead of time. You're not the only one traveling to college the first week in September!

Airlines, railways, and bus companies often offer bargain fares if you are willing to buy tickets in advance. This is one trip you definitely know you're taking, so make arrangements early, save some money, and cross that item off your list.

Are you driving to school? If the family car won't hold you, whoever is going with you, and all your gear, consider borrowing or renting a station wagon, small van, or U-Haul truck or trailer. Again, make arrangements as early as possible. This is the season for moving and the rental vehicle you need may not be available when you need it unless you reserve it in advance.

Don't Forget Your Parents!
Your parents won't have a dorm room waiting for them when you all arrive at college. Unless they're going right home, they'll need a place to stay. So will everybody else's parents. Most colleges supply a listing of local accommodations. These fill up very quickly. So if your folks are staying over, reserve early so they don't spend your first night at college driving around trying to find a bed.

Packing Up
You'll probably take most of your stuff with you if you are driving to school. If you don't drive, you'll have to

Travel Plans Checklist

Yours

Air/Bus/Train _____

Terminal _____

Date _____

Departure time _____

Arrival time _____

Flight No. _____

Cost _____

Rental Arrangements

Station wagon _____ Van _____ U-Haul _____

Pick up from _____

Pick up time _____

Return to _____

Return time _____

Cost _____

Your Parents'

Hotel Name _____

Address _____

Phone _____

Date(s) booked _____

Cost _____

Travel Plans Checklist

Your Gear

College mailing address ————————————————

————————————————————————————

————————————————————————————

————————————————————————————

To be sent via ——————————————————————

Mailing date ————————————————————————

For complete packing lists, see pages 89–90.

Notes and Deadlines

————————————————————————————

————————————————————————————

————————————————————————————

————————————————————————————

————————————————————————————

————————————————————————————

————————————————————————————

————————————————————————————

————————————————————————————

————————————————————————————

————————————————————————————

————————————————————————————

ship most of it ahead and travel with a couple of suitcases, a duffel bag, or a backpack.

If the material your college sends you does not
make clear when packages can be accepted at the dormitory and *exactly* how they should be addressed, call
the housing office or your dorm counselor to find out.
You can usually figure that it will take a minimum of
three to five days for packages to arrive and as long as
two to three weeks, depending on distance and type of
shipping service used. (See "Packing Tips" in Chapter
3 for more information.)

Clothes Shopping Strategies

Putting together a college wardrobe is usually done in
fits and starts. You may go out determined to buy everything on your list from belts to boots, but after six
hours of schlepping you have one Shetland sweater,
one pair of running shoes, and one pair of parrot ear-
rings. You found a down jacket you loved but they
didn't have it in your size, the corduroy pants you
craved only came in a disgusting shade of brown, and
your mother said that the price tag on the only dress
you liked equaled your entire clothing allowance.

Shopping can be a trying experience for both you
and your parent, but with good will and a little pre-
planning, you can negotiate this particular minefield.
Here are some strategies to keep in mind:

- Set a budget. Determine, before your first shopping
  expedition, how much you have to spend on your
  college wardrobe. (However, if you shop with your
  mother and see two terrific sweaters, she might be
  willing to stretch the budget and say, "Take them
  both, dear.")

- Review your current wardrobe. Check your closets and drawers to see what's there. Then, when your mother says, "I thought you *had* a navy pleated skirt," you can honestly say that you don't. Knowing what's in your closet will also help you to co-ordinate your new black leather pants with your old gray silk blouse.

- Make a specific shopping list. Don't just write "shirt" when what you need is a long-sleeved white button-down shirt, or "underwear" when what you need are six pairs of boxers or underpants and a jogging bra.

- Avoid a shopping marathon. Take time out when you know you're getting tired. Lunch or a cup of tea can do wonders for you after you've tried on seventeen sweaters and bought none of them. It can also revive your weary mother who has said, "That's lovely, darling," seventeen times.

- Take an enthusiastic shopper with you. If your mother hates shopping, or you and she are not on the same wavelength, go with somebody else. You can probably think of some dedicated shopper—an aunt, cousin, or friend—who would enjoy going with you. Some stores have personal shoppers who can help you find the kind of clothes you're looking for in your price range.

After several shopping expeditions, you may find that you have acquired one parka, six pairs of sweat socks, and a down comforter. However, you still haven't found the perfect jeans jacket.

Before much more time elapses, you should probably go out and get sneakers, underwear, and sweatpants. As for the rest, you can wait until you get to college and buy the clothes you need once you check out the campus style.

Three Weeks Before You Leave

Check Your Equipment

The search for the perfect jeans jacket may continue, but this is the time to check your equipment. Is your typewriter in good working condition? You don't really want to go on typing without the letter "g" or making little holes in the paper every time you end a sentence. If your typewriter isn't in good working order, take it in for a cleaning and overhaul. If you are taking your computer, make sure you have discs, ribbons, and other supplies.

Does your tennis racket need restringing? Are your skis in shape? Is your Frisbee a has-been? Have you put off fixing your turntable since your graduation party? Do you plan to transfer all your records (and your brother's records) onto tape? Use the Equipment Checklist to keep track of these and other chores.

Two Weeks Before You Leave

The more information you can get about your room, the easier it is to decide what to take. If you haven't found out what size and shape your room is and what furnishings the college supplies, don't buy furnishings until you get there. You may need a floor lamp instead of a desk lamp; you may not need a mirror for over the dresser because there's one inside the closet door. One Harvard senior noted that it's worth investing in a few good things—a rug, a bookcase, a desk chair—because you'll be using them for four years.

Equipment Checklist

Typewriter

Date taken for repair: _____ Ready by:_____

Cost: _____ Picked up:_____

Computer

Supplies needed: _____

_____

_____

Sports Equipment

Item	Things to Do	Done
_____	_____	_____
_____	_____	_____
_____	_____	_____

Music Equipment

Item	Things to Do	Done
_____	_____	_____
_____	_____	_____
_____	_____	_____
_____	_____	_____

Some colleges provide an optional linen service, but most students bring their own pillows, linens, and blankets. Make sure your sheets will fit your mattress: Some rooms have mattresses that need "twin extra-long" sheets.

Preparing to Pack

When you tuck your comforter at the bottom of a box, under your hair dryer and some underwear, you know exactly where it is. But a week or so later, faced with three identical boxes, will you know which one has the comforter?

Use the "Packing Checklists" at the end of this chapter to write down what you are packing where. We don't know if you're using a trunk, liquor cartons, large plastic garbage bags, or matching monogrammed luggage to get your stuff to school, so we call them "Boxes." Number your boxes as you fill them.

Moving-In Day Checklist

_____ Basic tool kit. You're going to need the following items so that you can hang a mirror, remove old nails, and put up a hook for your bathrobe.
- Hammer
- Nails
- Screwdriver
- Staple gun
- Thumbtacks

_____ Tape. Double-faced tape is ideal for hanging up posters, especially in dorms where they don't allow you to hammer nails into the walls. Regular cellophane tape is useful if you tear a book cover or a photograph.

_____ Extension cords and multiple electric outlets. There are never enough electrical outlets (and they're always in the wrong place) for you to plug in two lamps, a stereo, and your clock radio, not to mention your computer, your electric pencil sharpener, and your fan.

_____ Tape measure. Before you rush out to buy a bookcase to fit between your bed and your desk, it's important to know exactly how wide the space is. An under-bed storage box doesn't work if it doesn't fit under your bed. And if the sun is pouring in and you need a window shade, you can't buy one without knowing the width and length of the window.

_____ Key ring. When you arrive, somebody is going to give you a key to your room, a key to your dorm, and a key to your mailbox. You're likely to lose them if they're floating around loose in your pocket, so put them on a key ring. Then you can lose them all at once!

_____ Garbage bags. A couple of those big, heavy-duty garbage bags gives you somewhere to throw the stuff your parents don't want to lug home again and the remnants of cardboard, paper, and cord that accumulate as you unpack.

_____ Notebook and pencil. These are for making a shopping list of the odds and ends you have to go out and get—like a three-way light bulb for your lamp, or a laundry bag.

_____ Pair of scissors or sharp knife. You'll need a cutting tool to open the boxes you sealed so carefully with super-duper strong tape.

> Remember where you put the keys to your cases or trunk after you lock them up. Take the keys with you. Don't leave them at home on your dresser!

One Week Before You Leave

Saying Good-bye

Now is the time to say good-bye to all the people you won't be seeing for a while. Even students who are going to college only an hour away from home feel an irrepressible urge to hug their friends one last time, although they know they're going to see each other in a couple of months.

You want to say good-bye to the gang at the store where you worked. You want to say good-bye to your buddies on the soccer team. You want to say good-bye to the teacher who ran the drama department. There's the family you baby-sat for all through high school. And what about your grandparents in Vermont, who have offered to pay your way if you'll come to visit before you take off?

Dolores, now a senior at Bowdoin, remembers the frantic good-byes before she left for Maine. "I ran around like a chicken with its head cut off," she said. "Thinking back, it was a little silly. I really only wanted to say good-bye to a few good friends, but I felt as if I had to see everybody."

If you think you might forget someone, make a list of the people you want to call or see before you leave.

The Last Few Days

Don't lie awake at night worrying that you've bought the wrong clothes or haven't got enough. Maybe you'll find the ideal jeans jacket once you get to college. At least you discovered the perfect down vest in the Army and Navy store—and it was on sale. And your cousin sent you a clock radio, so you can cross that off your list. The flexibility to fill in gaps in your wardrobe and room furnishings can be a blessing in disguise—who knows what great stuff you'll find where you're going?

The stuff you're sending—linens, clothing, books—has to be packed up, labeled, and sent off in time to arrive before you do. On that first night in the dorm, when you're ready to fall into bed after an exhausting and exciting day, you don't want to have to hunt through all your boxes looking for your sheets. That's when you'll be glad you filled in those packing lists.

Pack what you think you'd like to have for the first couple of days in the suitcases you take with you. If you go by car with your parents, you can unpack as soon as you get there and let your parents bring home the empty baggage. But be sure to keep one small case or duffel for traveling and going home for the weekend.

Right now, you're full of good intentions to keep in touch with your relatives and friends. Be sure you have an up-to-date address book so you won't have to phone home every time you want to write or call someone.

If you are going by plane, train, or bus and haven't already picked up your tickets, do so now. Picking them up the day you leave is a hassle you can do without.

If you are renting a station wagon or U-Haul, pick it up the day before you leave so you can get packed up and ready to go first thing in the morning. It's not a good idea to leave a loaded vehicle on the street, so you'll want to get up early; it takes time to fit you, your family, your gear, your skis, your stuffed animals, and your younger sister into the car.

Just to be on the safe side, when you go to get gas, check the tires, oil, and water.

It's the Night Before College

And all through the house, there's anxiety and nostalgia. Your mother can't believe you're old enough to go to college; your father can't believe everything will fit into the car; your sister can't believe you're so mean that you'd take your Springsteen records before she had a chance to tape them; your grandparents call to complain that they can't believe you never found the time to come see them.

You're probably in great shape, but the night before a big move is inevitably a bit frantic. You've got to run a load or two through the washing machine. The phone doesn't stop ringing. You'd love to meet your friends at the diner, but your folks seem to think you should spend the evening with them.

It's understandable that everyone is a little on edge. Most freshmen tell us that they kept worrying about what they had forgotten. Chances are that you will remember to pack your toothbrush; however, if you don't—trust us! They have toothbrushes where you're going. Toothpaste, too.

Your parents won't disown you if you leave your room looking as though a cyclone passed through. However, it's a nice gesture to leave your bed made, throw out the tattered magazines, and clear the left-behind clothes off the floor.

Packing Checklists

BOX #1
Contains _____

_____

_____

_____

_____

_____

_____

BOX #2
Contains _____

_____

_____

_____

_____

_____

_____

BOX #3
Contains _____

_____

_____

_____

_____

_____

_____

Packing Checklists

BOX #4
Contains _____
_____
_____
_____
_____
_____
_____
_____

BOX #5
Contains _____
_____
_____
_____
_____
_____
_____

BOX #6
Contains _____
_____
_____
_____
_____
_____
_____

The First Few Days

After the ecstasy of acceptance and the agony of anticipation, the first day of college finally dawns.

It also dawns for the 2,321 other freshmen in your class and, what is more, they all decide to arrive at the same time you do. Like you, they need to unload their boxes, shopping bags, tennis rackets, standing lamps, and suitcases; haul them up the stairs or into the only working elevator; and dump everything into a room that was designed to hold at best a fraction of this stuff.

Their parents, like yours, are anxiously trying to help, and keep asking questions like, "Did you remember to bring your umbrella?"—which, of course, you deliberately left behind.

Every college develops a system to make arrival day less chaotic. For example, some schools allow only a limited number of cars to park in front of a dorm for a limited period of time. Others tell students to arrive at specific times during the course of the day. And some schools provide luggage handcarts, which always disappear within the first hour.

Nothing really helps. Just try to keep your cool and muddle through with as good grace as you can manage. Wear something comfortable—this is not the day to establish your sartorial brilliance. And remember, as Scarlett O'Hara was wont to say, "After all, tomorrow is another day."

There's no need to do everything at once. For now, just get your belongings into your room, which is always bigger or smaller, more or less crowded, lighter or darker than you had imagined.

Freshman Orientation

Freshman orientation is unlike any other experience in your college life. It is a specially planned introduction to the university community and your classmates before your first class even starts.

Each college offers a different orientation program. Some last a few days, and some go on for a week. Some programs encourage parents to attend at least part of the time and provide special seminars for them.

One parent remembers: "On arrival day we assembled outside in the main quadrangle. The dean of our son's college welcomed all the new students and parents and pointed out that some kids were probably worrying that they didn't really belong there. He assured them the Admissions Committee knew what it was doing."

The goal of all these programs is to help you feel at home on campus and to get to know a lot of other freshmen who are just as apprehensive as you are.

Freshman orientation is designed to flood you with information. There may be campus tours and slide shows. There may be visits to the different libraries. There will be meetings with dorm counselors, faculty members, deans, and representatives of university offices so that you get to meet some of the professors and administrative staff. There may be performances by singing groups. Registration materials will be distributed, and at some schools you will register for your first courses. Many schools have a computerized registration system that will be explained to you.

At orientation, you'll find it very hard to avoid

meeting dozens of other freshmen—over the buffet out-side the observatory, munching hamburgers and hot dogs at the student center cookout, at the all-day open house complete with pizza and ice cream.

At Haverford College, for example, freshman orien-tation includes a tour of the arboretum, an evening of college songs and skits, a picnic lunch with faculty advisers, night Frisbee golf, a Bugs Bunny film festival, interdorm Olympics (a note advises "You will get wet!!"), planting the class tree, and taking the class picture.

You'll certainly find someone to talk to at the barbe-cue, the square dance, or lying in the sun outside your dorm. Every college group from the Asian-American Student Association to the Students Against Apart-heid, from the Women's Golf Club to the Amateur Radio Society will be competing for your attention.

The orientation schedule is deliberately designed to be extraordinarily hectic, but you'll still find time—maybe at two in the morning!—to discuss the pressing problems facing the free world or what your parents will say if you come home with your ears pierced.

Living with a Roommate, or Two or Three

You may think you've avoided roommate problems be-cause you met this really nice freshman from Santa Bar-bara at orientation and you both decided it would be fun to share a room. So you requested each other on the form the college provided and you're looking forward to living together.

Or, like most freshmen, you've been assigned a roommate or two. Perhaps now that you have three names you're in a mild panic because you're an only child and have never shared a room with anyone.

Perhaps you and your assigned roommate have talked on the phone and it seems as though everything's going to work out. But the day you move into the minuscule living space you're supposed to share, you take one look at each other and you both realize that someone has made a terrible mistake.

If you're very lucky, your freshman roommate may turn out to be one of your best friends. Some seniors on campus have coexisted happily with their randomly assigned roommates for four years. If this happens to you, terrific!

But if you find that the person with whom you share your cozy room is driving you bananas because you can't stand each other's music, viewpoints, friends, or personal habits, don't feel that your only option is to grit your teeth, suffer in silence, and withdraw.

Problems crop up in unexpected places. You may share his taste in music, but grow to loathe his computer. A Clark University housing director said, "If there's a real serious hacker who keeps the screen on all night and it winks and beeps and the other person wants to sleep, you get fairly predictable reactions."

You are not the first freshman in history to find yourself living with someone you don't get along with, and there are lots of ways to improve the situation.

At Penn State, a Roommate Starter Kit distributed to all freshmen encourages them to sit down at the very beginning with their new roommates and discuss everything under the sun. They talk about attitudes toward drugs, alcohol, sex, and religion. They also talk about their homes, their parents, brothers and sisters, and friends from high school. They air their opinions on music, on how much sleep they need, on study habits and housekeeping standards.

Many other schools provide booklets, and use meetings, role playing, and games to help new students adjust to living with other people. One Tufts senior said, "I learned to say to my roommate, 'Please turn down your stereo . . . I can't study', instead of blaring back with my own stereo."

Some disagreements are inevitable when people from different backgrounds find themselves sharing living space. The central idea behind all of these "getting to know you" programs is that roommates don't have to be soulmates, but they should be able to get along. Talking freely, sharing opinions, and working out ways to handle conflicts does not require that people *like* each other. And even if you and your roommates get along really well, you'll still have to negotiate some issues—like overnight guests and cleaning up. It's important to know how to tell your roommate that last night's leftover pizza under his bed really bugs you.

You don't want to find yourself avoiding your own room. If you can learn some techniques for resolving these kinds of problems, you'll have learned an important lesson.

"My roommate," recalled Michael, a student at Washington State, "really geared up around midnight. I'm a crew jock who had to be on the river at six every morning. For weeks I tried to sleep through the telephone calls, the visitors, and the country music. Finally, I talked to him. He was genuinely surprised: He had no idea how I felt. He actually thought I was sleeping through it all. We agreed that he'd go over to his friends after eleven, and I took the phone off the hook."

Michael might have saved himself a lot of aggravation if, instead of stewing silently, he and his roommate had taken the time to talk it out sooner.

Compatibility Quotient

Some counselors actually recommend that students write and sign a "contract" covering how they plan to handle a variety of issues—such as how to arrange the furniture, how much noise is tolerable, what time to go to bed. They feel a written agreement is a commitment and not so easy to go back on.

Joanne Soliday, Dean of Admissions and Financial Planning at Elon College in North Carolina, emphasizes: "What you need to do is decide ahead of time what will and will not occur in your room. You're smart enough to go to college, but you need to be strong enough to stand up for yourself and your beliefs." To help you sort out what's important to you and your roommate(s), determine possible typical friction points by using the "Compatibility Checklist." Any issue on which you and your roommate are far apart is worth discussing before it becomes a crisis.

Three Steps to Working Things Out

Negotiation
You like your day to begin to the strains of soft rock from your clock radio. You're surprised to discover that music in the morning sets your roommate's teeth on edge. Time to negotiate.

Maybe you're in a triple and your two roommates like the room hot as a sauna. You want the windows open all the time, but especially when you go to bed. Time to negotiate.

Assess how important each issue is to each of you. You may have to give up soft rock in the morning. Your roommates may have to agree to one open window by your bed.

Compatibility Checklist

	Important to you	Important to your roommate(s)
Music in the morning	————	————
Music in the evening	————	————
Watching television	————	————
A neat room	————	————
A clean room	————	————
Open windows	————	————
Having visitors over	————	————
Having overnight guests	————	————
Studying in room	————	————
Borrowing/lending	————	————
Taking messages	————	————
Smoking in the room	————	————
Alcohol in the room	————	————
Swearing	————	————

Other issues that are important to you:

_____	————	————
_____	————	————
_____	————	————

Rate these issues on a scale of 1 (who cares?) to 5 (crucial!).

Other issues that you might want to discuss are: when room-mates usually go to bed, when they will be getting up, how the room should be decorated, who can use your computer, who will work out the phone bill each month, etc.

"These negotiating skills are useful in many situations," points out Barbara Engram in Hood College's *Roommate Negotiation Workbook.* "You and your roommate share a living space, but there will be many other times when you will share space with someone. Skill in reaching agreements about behavior in a shared space will help you to manage your relationships more effectively and pleasantly."

Mediation

You can't stand it when your roommate's boyfriend stays all night. You've tried talking to her, but she laughs and says you'll get used to him. Negotiation has failed: What to do?

This is the moment to look beyond the two of you for an outside person to mediate. Arrange for a meeting in which your dorm counselor—or someone else you and your roommate both trust—hears both sides of the issue. You won't be as likely to dismiss each other's concerns when somebody else is involved in the discussion. The mediator may suggest a solution you haven't thought of. And describing your problem to an outsider can help both of you deal with the issue in a less personal way: You recognize that you're arguing about how late visitors can stay and not about which of you is more "rotten, mean, and spoiled." Mediation is a logical next step when negotiation breaks down.

Arbitration

Let's say your roommate is really a turkey. She refuses to negotiate; she won't meet with you and your dorm counselor. Her boyfriend has moved in for the duration. What can you do next?

Your dorm counselor can act as an arbitrator and consult with you and your roommate separately to suggest a course of action. The essence of arbitration is that you both agree to abide by the arbitrator's decision. In one extreme instance, a young woman who refused to be parted from her boyfriend moved out of the dorm altogether.

Finding Your Way Around

The first time you make your way from your dorm to the dining hall to the student union to the library, you can, like Hansel and Gretel in the forest, leave a trail of bread crumbs so you can make your way back. But that's not practical. So admit you're a freshman and take along the map from your orientation packet. You'll soon identify the quickest route between the gym and the bookstore, locate the shuttle bus stops, and find out where the computer center is.

Safety Alert

A college campus in the daytime feels pretty safe. If you come from a big city, a tree-lined quad looks like a paradise of peace and quiet. Unfortunately, colleges are not isolated from the rest of the world, and statistics show there are rapes, robberies, and violence in even the most idyllic settings.

Colleges are aware these problems exist and have introduced a range of safety measures. For example, entrance doors to dorms are kept locked and you can only get in with a key or, if you're visiting, you phone up and a resident lets you in.

At night, special police patrol the campus and students are advised to use designated travel routes. Often there are clearly marked emergency telephones that connect you directly to security services without dialing. Many colleges offer escort services to accompany students who would otherwise have to walk home alone after a late night at the language lab or computer center. At the University of Virginia, for instance, a student watch service with personnel carrying flashlights and radios patrols the central campus area keeping an eye out for any suspicious activities or persons.

You never believe anything's going to happen to you. But the sad fact is that there are people in this world whom you don't want to meet at midnight in the narrow alleyway two blocks from your dorm. Be chicken on this one—walk in well-lighted areas where there are likely to be other students, and make use of the security services.

Food for Thought

Beware the Freshmen Ten!

Those Freshmen Ten are the pounds you're likely to gain if you fall into the snack-as-you-go pattern. You may pick them up eating at odd hours—after all, if you finish dinner at seven and you're up studying at two, hunger pangs can attack.

The Freshman Ten sneak up on you as you finish off the chocolate chip cookies your roommate's mother sent, send out for pizza four nights in a row, and create a new flavor extravaganza at the blend-in ice cream parlor. And while the dining hall and snack bar are great places to hang out, watch it! While you're shooting the breeze, you may be stuffing your face.

In the olden days (when your parents went to college), college dining rooms served fixed menus at fixed times and if you didn't like the food or arrived late, too bad. Today, colleges offer choices that range from croissants to crabcakes. Students are better informed about nutrition, so most dining halls have a salad bar and offer meals with chicken, pasta, yogurt, and fresh fish, as well as the traditional pizza, hamburgers, and french fries.

These days, you get to pick what you want to eat. At Manhattanville College, students who get up early can make their own waffles or poach eggs in a do-it-yourself egg cooker. Pancakes, french toast, bacon, ham, or sausage are on the menu, too.

Although students still drink a lot of soda, milk and juice are increasingly popular. Some dining services offer special menus of dishes prepared with polyunsaturated fats and low-fat dairy products.

You know that a balanced diet includes the four food groups—dairy products; fruit and vegetables; whole grains and cereals; and meat, fish, and chicken. Your parents told you. You heard it in high school. You probably read it in newspapers and magazines. It's booooooooring . . . but it's true. If you eat right, you'll feel right.

Recognizing Eating Disorders

There's a clear line between wanting to lose those ten pounds that crept up on you during your first semester, and serious eating disorders like anorexia nervosa and bulimia.

Colleges now realize that many young people, particularly women, suffer from these diseases. On a national level, hundreds of thousands of women in their teens and twenties experience severe eating disorders.

Anorexia nervosa is a form of severe, deliberate self-starvation, from which some people die and others do extreme, sometimes irreparable, damage to their bodies. Symptoms include an obsession with how much food is eaten, feelings of inferiority, and deluded thinking about body size.

People with *bulimia* don't starve themselves: They binge on large quantities of food and then purge their systems with laxatives and vomiting. These people typically eat a lot very rapidly and then induce vomiting. At the other extreme, they will fast for extended periods.

"When we began to see students with clear eating disorders, we set up programs to help them," said a college physician. "These kids require a combination of psychological and physiological support. The hardest part is getting them to admit they have a problem."

Some colleges have hot lines or clinics that deal with eating disorders. Others handle them through health services. If you suspect a friend is suffering from one of these disorders, talk to your dorm counselor.

7

Who Can Answer My Questions?

"When you're at college, no one's going to knock on your door and ask if you need any help, especially in big schools," said Will, who just graduated from the University of Wisconsin, remembering how overwhelmed he was during his first weeks. "I was off the wall when I went to a counselor and told him how much I hated calculus. He told me to drop it and take courses I liked in my first semester. And he was totally right. What a relief!"

Colleges offer lots of information and services to help incoming students, but it can be tricky plugging into them. After a little while you'll learn to find your way through what may seem at first like a maze of college administration offices, academic departments, and student services.

Finding Out About Everything

Every college has its own system. For example, the University of New Mexico has a 24-hour-a-day telephone information service with over 200 topics of interest to students, as well as a "Telemessage"—a recording outlining resources on campus.

Your college provides a student handbook or a freshman guide detailing the resources, courses, services, and information available. You may receive a monthly activity calendar, a guide to student organizations, a campus map, a copy of your college newspaper. Most schools have a centrally located information center.

This chapter will help you pinpoint the resources you need and keep track of the names and phone numbers of people you contact. Don't make the mistake of thinking that colleges are not prepared to deal with your special problems: There's probably somebody on campus assigned to help you. For example, like many other schools, the University of Delaware has special services and programs for disabled students, including classroom note takers and assistance in locating tutors.

Don't think it's a sign of immaturity to ask for help. On the contrary, recognizing that you need help and going to get it is a sign of maturity. Often, though, it's a good idea to call first so you end up in the right office talking to the right person.

Keeping Track of Whom to Contact

Housing

As a freshman, you'll probably be living in a dorm. If you have questions or problems, contact:

Office of Residential Life/Housing Office

Name _____

Address _____

Phone _____

A dorm counselor, usually an upperclassman, is assigned to your residence.

Dorm Counselor _____

Phone _____

If your room is next to the bathroom and the comings and goings keep you up all night, or if your roommate is driving you crazy, call:

Housing Office/Dorm Counselor _____

Phone _____

When you look up at the ceiling and have the impression it's about to fall down, contact:

Dormitory Damage and Maintenance _____

Phone _____

Most freshmen eat in dining halls in or near their dorms. If you have a question about where or what to eat, or if you have special food requirements—vegetarian, kosher, nondairy, low sodium, or whatever—call:

Dining Services _____

Phone _____

Financial Arrangements
Money and finances are covered in detail in Chapter 4. If you have a question or problem, the initial person to contact is usually the registrar.

Registrar

Name _____

Address _____

Phone _____

Financial Aid Office/Bursar's Office

Name _____

Address _____

Phone _____

Loans and Scholarships

Name _____

Address _____

Phone _____

Student Employment Office

Name _____

Address _____

Phone _____

Off-Campus Job Placement

Name _____

Address _____

Phone _____

It's helpful to know someone at your friendly local bank for the times you may be overdrawn or for the day a check doesn't arrive in time.

Your Bank

Name _____

Manager _____

Address _____

Phone _____

Account Number _____

Do you plan to get an instant cash card? If you think you'll forget your code identification, make a note of it somewhere—in a place you'll remember and nobody else knows.

In case they're lost or stolen, note your credit card numbers.

Credit Cards

Name and Number _____

_____

_____

Academic Matters

Every college has deans who are responsible for a different area of student life. Your dorm counselor understands how the university works and can help you identify the person who can help you.

Advanced Placement Credits

Whom to call: _____

Phone _____

Academic Standing

Whom to call: _____

Phone _____

Academic Grievances

Whom to call: _____

Phone _____

At some point you will talk to:

Your Faculty Adviser

Name _____

Address _____

Phone _____

Dean of Your College (Arts and Sciences, Engineering, etc.)

Name _____

Address _____

Phone _____

Dean of Students

Name _____

Address _____

Phone _____

Dean of Freshmen

Name _____

Address _____

Phone _____

Course Scheduling and Career Planning

> Parents, who have had to take out large loans, look at their children as an investment. This makes students frantically take economics courses and others that look like career training. It's sad if this is not what really interests them. But it's hard to be high-minded with a $20,000 loan hanging over your head and your parents asking, "Why are you taking philosophy?"
> —Erica Wonnacott, Dean of Students,
> Middlebury College, Vermont

You may think you want to be a lawyer, and plan a program of prelaw courses. Your parents are delighted because you seem to know what you want to do, and they encourage you to stick with your chosen career path.

But watch it—you are cheating yourself if you arrive at college with blinkers on. Don't close the door on taking the creative writing course that sounds terrific. Be adventurous and take some side trips into new areas—perhaps anthropology, or linguistics, or Afro-American history.

You don't have to lock yourself into a career decision as soon as you arrive on campus. You may have always wanted to be a veterinarian, but discover that you enjoy and excel in ancient history. College is about possibilities.

If you take time to look into it, you'll find there's a great deal of flexibility. You can arrange a double major, for example, and take courses in two fields to gain expertise in both. You can use summer and winter breaks for jobs or internships that interest you. Don't load up your schedule with all the classes required for a particular major before you declare it—unless you want to take them anyway. It's not a sign of failure to change your major or career plans.

Ernest L. Boyer, author of a Carnegie Foundation survey of college undergraduates, stated: "In their search for a secure future, students have read the signals too literally. They have too often shunned the liberal arts courses altogether and focused only on a specialty. Rather than view a major as competing with a general education, these two essential parts of the bachelor's program should be intertwined. Otherwise, students will become technicians with no social perspective."

Every college has career planning services, sometimes several kinds. As an incoming freshman, you don't need career workshops, career counseling, career forums, company informational presentations, the career resource library, résumé-writing workshops, graduate school catalogs, or access to current job listings. When the time comes, you'll find your way to the office that has the information you need.

Dr. Nannerl Keohane, president of Wellesley College, puts it best: "College is one of the few times in your life when you can study what really turns you on."

Personal Counseling

The Freshman Nightmare: You are alone in your tiny room. You have no friends. No one calls you on your newly installed telephone. Everybody in your classes is smarter than you are. You are desperately homesick. You've gained six pounds in two weeks. And you are developing an excruciating earache.

What are you going to do? For these and other personal problems, there's somebody who can help. Your job is to reach out and tell someone. Probably the first person you should talk to is your dorm counselor.

For an earache, a bad cold, stomach cramps, or a pain that doesn't go away, visit:

Student Health Services

Name _____

Address _____

Phone _____

If you're feeling homesick, isolated, and generally depressed (which happens to a lot of freshmen in their first few weeks away from family and old friends), peer counseling can help you.

Student-to-Student Counseling

Name _____

Address _____

Phone _____

If your problems seem too weighty for another student, even an older, more experienced one, don't hesitate to seek out professional counseling from a trained psychologist.

Psychological Services

Name _____

Address _____

Phone _____

Some people find it easier to discuss their personal problems with a religious adviser.

Religious Counseling/Chaplain's Office

Name _____

Address _____

Phone _____

Student Activities

Almost anything you can think of, somebody has thought of already and there's a club, a team, a group, an association, a publication, a society, a committee, a coalition, or a network waiting for you.

Most campuses have a daily or weekly newspaper, a radio station, and maybe a TV station run by students. You can join a dance club or a student political organization or work for nuclear disarmament. Is it to be Ultimate Frisbee, the Film Society, or a fraternity? Have you always wanted to be a cheerleader? To play chess?

There are social and political organizations for almost every racial, ethnic, religious, and sexual point of view. And there may even be some unique special interest groups on your campus—like RASP (Redheads Are Special People), created to unite the redheaded student body at one eastern college, or the cricket team you can join at another university.

The Student Union or Student Activities Office coordinates many of these activities and maintains an up-to-date list of whom to call if you're interested in participating. The Athletic Department coordinates intercollegiate and intramural sports programs.

Student Union/Student Activities Office

Address _____

Phone _____

Athletic Department

Address _____

Phone _____

I'm interested in:

Activity _____

Address _____

Phone _____

Activity _____

Address _____

Phone _____

Activity _____

Address _____

Phone _____

Activity _____

Address _____

Phone _____

Settling In

Y ou've unpacked, your bed is made, your Picasso poster is up, and your parents have gone home. If you're thinking that college wasn't such a good idea after all, you're not alone. Whether they admit it or not, many other freshmen feel just as queasy as you do.

Despite how you feel, you don't have to deal with everything today—or even tomorrow. In your first few weeks, you'll take it step by step—from registering for a course in Native-American Religions (and then dropping it because it meets at eight in the morning) to trying out for the dorm volleyball team (and making it) to getting a haircut (which you don't like much, but it'll grow out).

Most freshmen, even those who thought they couldn't wait to get away from home, feel homesick. It's painful, it's normal, and it goes away. The prescription is to keep busy, join at least one extracurricular activity, and get to know as many people as you can.

New Faces

Maybe you arrived at your state university with a whole bunch of other kids from your high school class. So at least you know somebody—and the temptation is to stick together for comfort and safety. But making new friends doesn't mean you have to give up your old ones.

You didn't come to college to recreate your high school experience. "I tell kids," said a high school counselor, "that every freshman is a new kid on the block. If

119

you can say, 'Hi, I'm Jeff from Cleveland, who are you?' you've taken an important first step."

Whether you're starting kindergarten, college, a new job, or moving to a new town, getting to know people takes time and effort. The first rule for making friends is: try not to eat alone. If you don't see a single familiar face in the cafeteria, introduce yourself to someone you don't know. That's one sure way of converting strangers to acquaintances, and some are likely to become friends. Take a chance and reach out—volunteer for the dorm social committee, for example. You will get to know who's in your dorm as you organize refreshments for the fall football party and may even find three other musicians as interested in forming a jazz combo as you are. Instead of huddling in your room complaining about how cold and snowy it is, try cross-country skiing and make friends with the other snow bunnies. Do you love the theater? You don't have to be a star—all companies need producers, lighting and sound technicians, stage designers and scenery painters, as well as people to help with publicity and ticket sales. You'll be pleasantly surprised at how many connections you can make once you begin.

Remembering Names

In your first few weeks you're going to be deluged with new people. They all have names, and you're going to forget some of them. Here are a few tips to help you put the face and the name together:

- Look directly at the person when you're introduced, and listen very hard to the name. Repeat it aloud.

- Link the name to someone you know with the

same name. For instance, connect someone named Washington with the first president.

- Define and visualize names like Walker, Taylor, Schumaker by occupation, and names like Ball, Field, and Green by the images they represent.

If you do find yourself talking to someone whose name you can't remember, the smartest solution is to smile and admit it.

Instant Best Friends

Making an instant best friend is a long shot. "I met Connie my very first day," said Jeannie, a freshman at Colorado State, "and she wanted us to do everything together. I'm kind of shy and she seemed to know her way around, so I went along. But we really didn't like the same things—she never wanted do what I wanted to do. When I wasn't willing to tag along with her, she got mad."

It takes time to find the people who will become your good friends, but you will.

Coping with Freshman Shock

This syndrome is not listed in any medical encyclopedia, but it's real. Freshman life is rife with unnerving moments.

These are some of the situations that can result in classic Freshman Shock. If you recognize them, you should be able to forestall a full-blown panic attack.

- You go to Freshman Convocation, look around, and realize that you don't know a soul.

- You come from a small, rural high school. You walk into your first class and see five hundred students crowding into the lecture hall.

- You were president of your senior class, captain of the soccer team, and founder of an interschool committee to help the homeless. Suddenly you're a lowly freshman and nobody knows or cares what a big shot you were.

- You walk across campus to the library and not one single person says hello.

- You check out the dining hall and don't see anybody to sit with.

- You never got anything lower than a B in your life. You get your first history paper back and it's a C.

- You were editor of your high school paper, so you decide to go out for the college daily. At the first meeting, you realize that every other freshman in the room was editor of the high school paper.

- You were an alternate on your high school tennis team. You watch varsity tennis team tryouts and consider taking up needlepoint.

- You wake up with a stuffy nose and a sore throat and suspect you have a fever. The windows are covered with frost. Nobody comes to take your temperature, nobody reminds you to wear a sweater, and nobody offers to drive you to class.

There is no instant relief for Freshman Shock. "I kept wondering what I was doing here," said Judy, a Bennington freshman. "I worried that soon I would really have to tell my folks I was never going to stick out four years of this."

Trust us. Things will get better.

- Enormous introductory courses are typical of large universities. If you arrive early enough to get a seat up front, you'll get to know some people in your class. Also, you'll have a better chance to talk to your professor or the instructor in the small sections that meet weekly. Later on, you'll find that the more advanced courses have fewer students.

- You may not spot many familiar faces in your first week. But as you hang out with the other freshman in your dorm, swap notes with your classmates, and talk to the person sitting across from you in the dining hall, you soon won't be able to walk across campus without meeting someone you know.

  "When my parents came up for Freshman Parents' Weekend in the middle of October, they were surprised at how many people said hello to me," said Dana, "and I realized I'd come to feel at home."

- You'll discover that competition in college is a lot stiffer than it was in high school. After all, you're competing with people whose SAT scores were as high as yours! That C on your first paper was a downer—but you can bet you weren't the only one to get a C. Do something: Go and see your professor or instructor and find out what your C means and what you can do to improve it.

  "When I got a low grade on my first English essay, I was devastated," said Carl. "I went to see my instructor and he told me that he liked to wake freshmen up by giving low grades." Your professor may suggest some remedial help or tutoring. Or this may be the first indication that history isn't your bag.

  "It's hard for a student who excelled in high school chemistry to discover she's only doing B or B minus work at college," said a science professor. "I advise them not to panic or bail out after a couple of low grades. One of the tasks students face at college is redefining their abilities."

- Similarly, it shouldn't come as a complete surprise that college varsity sports are extremely competitive. To give as many students as possible a chance to participate, most schools have sports clubs and intramurals. So if you don't excel at one sport, try another. Play on the dorm softball team, go swimming, try volleyball, go hiking.

- What about the glut of former editors trying out for the campus newspaper? You'll just have to do exactly what you did in high school—work your way up. Think about it this way: You'll be working with exciting, motivated people who will bring out the best in you.

- When you feel lousy, that's when the really big difference between living at home and being away at school hits you. When you're down, *you* have to do something about it—you don't have a parent to watch over you. You decide whether or not to go to class, you get yourself to student health, and you keep track of taking your medicine.

Every time you handle a problem on your own, you acquire assurance and a sense of your own competence. When you get your paper in on time even though you have a terrible cold and have broken up with your boyfriend or girlfriend, you'll feel pretty good about your ability to manage.

Don't be surprised to find that by the time you get totally comfortable being a freshman, you'll almost be a sophomore!

Oliver, a senior at Kenyon, said, "Freshmen need two things—a trusty alarm clock so they get up in time, and the ability to reinvent themselves every day as they keep meeting new people."

Getting to Know Yourself

You may want to change your image, your style, and your academic direction once you get to college—and you can if you want to. If you were a science and technology person in high school and want to try drama, this is your chance. On the other hand, if you've always enjoyed spending time with a few close friends, it's unlikely that you'll feel comfortable masquerading as the campus extrovert.

These contradictory options may be confusing, but finding the right balance is one of your important tasks in college.

"I hated living in a great big dorm—it was too impersonal and too noisy," explained Jay, now a junior at Syracuse. "My solution, sophomore year: I moved into a fraternity where I have a small room to myself and I've made some really good friends."

For others, dorm life is the perfect introduction to what college is all about. "I come from Brooklyn and I'm Jewish and had always lived in the city," said Marcia. "On my freshman corridor there was an aggie—an agricultural student—who'd grown up on a farm in Iowa. Because our backgrounds were so different, we found each other totally fascinating. If I'd just stuck with my old friends, I'd never have gotten to know anyone like her."

There are many ways to explore the wide range of people and activities available on campus and, in the process, learn more about yourself.

Religious Groups

Student religious groups on campus will welcome you. Besides services, they usually offer social events, discussion groups, and opportunities for community service.

At Harvard, for example, there is an astonishing diversity of religious activities. These include: Baha'i prayer meetings; Baptist, Christian Science, Congregational, Episcopal, Greek Orthodox, Hindu, Jewish, Lutheran, Methodist, Mormon, Roman Catholic, Quaker, and Unitarian services; as well as Humanist meetings and interfaith and interracial dialogues.

While many colleges don't have quite this much variety, you'll find a wide range of religious groups at whatever nondenominational college or university you attend. Check with the office of student activities to find out what services and events are scheduled regularly for your particular religion.

Ethnic and Other Groups

Whether or not to join an ethnic or special interest group is a question you're going to have to think through. Many campuses have organizations for black students, for gay students, for Korean students, for Native-American students, for Hispanic students, etc., which provide support and solidarity and, in the case of ethnic groups, enable students to enjoy the traditions of their common heritage.

On the other hand, these groups tend to isolate students from mainstream university life. If you do join one of these groups, you may want to strike a balance and join a more general interest group as well.

Fraternities and Sororities

Theoretically, all students are eligible to join fraternities and sororities, which are campus social groups usually affiliated with national Greek letter societies. Don't confuse these social groups with professional and honor societies with Greek alphabet names (like Phi Beta Kappa), for which you need professional credentials or demonstrated achievement.

Depending on what school you go to, fraternities and sororities may loom large or small or not at all. In colleges that have fraternities and sororities, Rush Week—the time when new members are recruited—occurs after orientation, sometimes during the first weeks of classes, or sometimes later on. You may wish you could delay the rush into rushing; however, at some schools, it's now or never. If you're ambivalent, talk to some upperclassmen who know the ropes.

At many schools, the pressure to join a fraternity or sorority can be intense. Belinda, a young woman at Southern Methodist University, characterized her experience as grueling: "Rush—the selection process sororities use to pick new members—begins with visiting a number of houses during Rush Week. Next, about half the rushees receive invitations to come back to parties where members put on skits and really focus on the freshmen they're most interested in. Then you make your list, in order of preference, of the sororities *you're* most interested in. The sororities make their cuts. If you're lucky, you're invited to a third round of parties. By this time there's a lot of anxiety wondering if you'll get a 'bid'—a formal invitation to join.

"After the final party, you sign a 'pref' card listing the sororities you'd be willing to pledge. The next day, if you're not going to get a bid, they call and let you know. If they don't call, you know you're in."

Belinda said that because she felt lonely living away from home, the sorority provided a family-like environment and a built-in social life. However, she admitted that sorority sisters tended to avoid friendships with students from different backgrounds.

Paul, who goes to a large Midwestern university, summed up the pros and cons: "When you join a fraternity right away, before you've had a chance to look around, you find instant friends. But then you're tied to these people. Later on you may want to break away, but it's hard. On the other hand, if the main social life on campus is at the fraternities, that's something you have to take into consideration."

Dealing with Emotional Ups and Downs

Settling in means redefining your relationship with your parents. Does your mother call every day and sometimes twice a day? Have your parents come to visit every weekend but one—and did you go home for that one?

"Some kids seem to be asking for this kind of attention," noted a psychologist in a college community. "But the message the parents give is that the kid can't manage on his or her own. Freshmen have to show they are developing an independent life at school with things to do that don't include their parents."

You don't want to hurt anybody's feelings, and you do need to keep in touch. Your parents should know what's going on in your life, and they can help you sort out your problems. It's reasonable to agree to call or write home once a week or so, and after a while you and your folks will find a comfortable pattern.

Lisa, an Oberlin sophomore, looked back at the first few weeks: "I called home, or wanted to, every single night. And then, after about a month, my folks called and wanted to know why they hadn't heard from me! I realized I'd been too busy to be homesick."

"My kids were always a bit miserable at first," said a mother of four grown children. "They couldn't wait to come back for Thanksgiving and see everyone. But after a couple of days here, they couldn't wait to get back to school. I went through this with the first two, so I didn't worry as much when the younger ones called and said they were lonely. I knew everything would be okay after Thanksgiving when they started to talk about going 'home' to college."

You're not the only one experiencing ups and downs in the first few weeks. Parents get confused, too. If you talk to your folks when you're at a low point, they imagine you are in the pits until you talk again. Parents eventually learn they get called when there's a crisis, but rarely when everything's going smoothly. Be the first kid on your block to share your good times as well as your difficult moments.

"When Ruth called one morning in tears, I tried to cheer her up," said her mother. "But I was depressed for the whole day, thinking about her being two hundred miles away from home. That evening, I called. She'd just come back from pizza and *The Rocky Horror Show* with friends and then, while she was doing her laundry, she met this great guy and they went out for coffee."

The other side of the coin is the parent who doesn't keep in touch. There are as many reasons for this as there are families, but the experience can be painful.

"My parents are divorced, my mother is in Italy, and my father is getting remarried," said Douglas. "Nobody even mentioned coming up for Freshman Parents'

Weekend. I sometimes call my dad but he's too busy to listen. Luckily for me, my roommate's parents have sort of adopted me."

This is one of those problems you won't know you have until it creeps up on you. If you are worried about a lack of contact with your folks, tell them. Or maybe talking to a counselor will help.

How Much Freedom Is Too Much?

You may already have a handbook with a complete listing of college policies. These regulations deal with issues like alcohol and how it is to be used on campus; dormitory damage; political activities; student businesses; campus security; fire safety; and smoking. They also spell out what is expected of you academically and ethically, and what happens if you cheat or plagiarize.

In spite of all the rules and regulations, you are going to have an enormous amount of freedom. This is the major hallmark marking the transition from high school senior to college freshman. For some kids, this liberty is intoxicating, and they respond with self-destructive and antisocial behavior. Others seize the opportunity to take responsibility for themselves and thrive on their new independence.

Drinking

Getting totally smashed isn't what it used to be . . . and it never was. There are rules about alcohol on campus, and each state establishes a legal drinking age. Drunken driving is dangerous to your health and to the health of those on the road with you.

College policies reflect the increasing awareness that alcohol is a drug and that addiction to alcohol is a major social problem. More and more schools encourage recreational activities that do not involve boozing it up. Several schools have chapters of Alcoholics Anonymous or run similar groups to help curb excessive drinking.

Drugs

They're illegal, which doesn't mean they're not available. One parent on a college tour asked the student guide, "Are there any problems with drugs on this campus?" The guide replied cheerfully, "No, not at all. You can get anything you want."

When you get to college, some kids will tell you that trying drugs is a sign of being grown-up. It's not. It's dumb and dangerous. If you or someone you know has a problem with drug abuse, the college health service can help you.

Sex

"When you're invited to a fraternity house, you often get taken on a tour," said Carole, a senior at the University of California. "And it always seems to end up in his bedroom. You should be prepared to deal with this."

On most campuses, you will encounter an atmosphere of sexual freedom. Today, many dorms are coed and nobody monitors your behavior. It's not like living at home and trying to find some private place to be with your boyfriend or girlfriend. At college, it's easy to be alone together. This means you must take full responsibility for your sexual behavior.

Most colleges offer medical care and professional counseling to help students cope with decisions about sexuality. These services go much further than just doling out information about birth control, because your sexuality is part of your total emotional, psychological, and physical make-up.

You have to work out your own guidelines, based on your religion, your upbringing, your needs, your convictions, and your attitude toward sex. Don't be pressured into doing anything you don't want to do.

Date rape—when somebody you know attacks you sexually—is a disturbing and often confusing issue. The man feels the woman led him on; the woman says they both had too much to drink, she tried to stop him, and he forced himself on her.

If a woman believes she was raped, she should report it or, at the very least, talk to a counselor who can help her decide what course of action to take and provide emotional support as well as objective advice. However, some women feel reluctant to press charges against men they know. The best defense is to be alert and avoid compromising situations.

Sexual harassment is usually an abuse of authority in which there is often an element of subtle or overt intimidation. It may be a male professor who keeps putting his hand on the knee of a female student who comes in for a conference: When she objects, he threatens to lower her grade. It may be a female professor who invites a male student to dinner and suggests they go to bed together: When he refuses, she tells him he'd better drop her class.

These examples are blatant and clear cut. Sometimes it's not so easy to be certain you are being harassed. If someone's behavior is bothering you, say so. If the behavior continues, that's harassment.

If you think you have a problem, you probably do. Talk to someone on the counseling staff who will keep the conversation confidential. You may find you're not the first person to encounter this kind of difficulty with this person. Write down exactly what happened and when, and save any notes or letters you receive.

Your next step, if the harassment continues, is to file a formal complaint, and your school should have a grievance procedure for dealing with harassment. In any case, a series of complaints about one professor will alert the administration. Colleges take seriously any harassment of their students. If charges are proved, a college will discipline and sometimes fire the offending staff member.

Doing What's Right for You

You are part of a generation that has grown up with an acceptance of premarital sex: Easy access to birth control is one reason, but there are many others, including the women's movement, which has encouraged men and women to recognize their sexual needs.

People mature at different rates. Men and women who do not feel ready for sexual involvement are right to wait. You may have already encountered sexual pressure in high school, and will almost certainly encounter more in college, but it's your body and your choice whether you say no or yes. The present AIDS epidemic has made this decision even more critical than it was in the past. If you do decide to say yes, it is essential to protect yourself.

Think about these issues now, before you find your-self in the middle of a passionate embrace. How do you feel about sex before marriage? What do you plan to do about birth control? In case of pregnancy, what would you do?

"Kids think they know a lot, but they don't know all the facts about sexually transmitted diseases like gonor-rhea, syphilis, and chlamydia," said a college physician. "AIDS has gotten a lot of attention, but that's not the only danger. Students tend to ignore problems related to sex until there's a crisis."

These problems are no fun. However, this chapter should provoke you into thinking about them. The de-cisions you make are important—and they'll affect the rest of your life.

Learning the Academic Ropes

You can develop a college schedule devoted to sleeping, eating, and playing—and you might be able to get away with it for a month or so. But this approach subverts your educational goals and is totally out of line with your dreams and your parents' ambitions for your future. It also seems counterproductive after all your efforts in high school to get into the college of your choice.

What Courses Do You HAVE to Take?

Let's face it, what you're going to do is comb through the course catalog and make some decisions. Don't feel you have to puzzle these out all by yourself. You should turn to your academic adviser, whose role is to help you figure out what courses to take; what the prerequisites are, if any; and what requirements you should get out of the way as early as possible. And you'll talk to other students.

You must earn a specific number of credits by completing course work to meet the requirements for your degree. During your college career, your courses will include prescribed subjects, often lumped together under a name like "core program" or "distribution requirements." You will probably choose courses under broad headings like: natural sciences, foreign languages, social and behavioral sciences, historical studies, and literature and fine arts. Every school has a different system for defining these major areas. However, the goal is always the same: to introduce you to diverse disciplines and give you a broad base for your later, more specialized studies.

137

Advanced Placement and Proficiency Exams

If you took Advanced Placement courses in high school and got high grades on the AP Examinations, you may be eligible for advanced placement in certain college departments. For example, you can earn course exemption or credit in biology, calculus, chemistry, computer science, English, music, physics, history, and foreign languages. These credits may enable you to graduate in fewer than four years or devote more time to specialized courses.

On the other hand, you may need remedial help. At the beginning of freshman year, you may be required to take placement tests to determine your proficiency in basic subject areas. If you score below a certain level, you may have to take a course to bring you up to the required level. For instance, many schools offer writing seminars for students whose writing skills need improvement. Some departments, like music and foreign languages, routinely require placement tests.

What Courses Do You WANT to Take?

"I wish I'd trusted my instincts more and taken creative writing courses early on," said Natasha, a senior at the University of Nebraska at Lincoln. "I think I was a little too afraid of being frivolous."

"I thought a course in Chinese Imaginative Literature would be really cool. Then I walked into the first lecture and found out it was in Chinese!" said Debra, a UCLA freshman.

Natasha and Debra are typical. The college catalog

is full of courses that sound fascinating. But the choices for freshmen are probably limited. Typically, there will be three required courses per semester— English, a foreign language, math or a science—and perhaps an introductory course for a possible major.

So what else should you take? Without exception, students will tell you to take whatever interests you. Which means that if you've always been fascinated by ancient Egyptian hieroglyphics or interested in the modern German cinema or concerned about the nuclear fuel cycle and the environment, this is your chance to learn all about it. "College is a great feast from which to choose," says an admissions dean at Stanford University. "Don't order the same meal every day."

Be as adventurous and ambitious as you can, without being unrealistic. Keep in mind as you go through the catalog that you don't want to overload your schedule with an impossible amount of required reading.

Who's Teaching the Course?

A course catalog can tell you only so much. It can't convey the quality of the teacher or the atmosphere in the classroom. Students who've already taken the course can fill you in.

Sometimes there's a guide that assesses the courses, based on student evaluations. Listings rate the professor, the course in general, the assigned reading, and the workload. These evaluations are subjective, and what you usually find are the extremes. The kids who respond tend to be those who really loathed the course and didn't do well, or those who really loved it and got a good grade.

Every school has its legendary professors, renowned for their ability to communicate their enthusiasm for their subjects. Don't miss these outstanding teachers, even if you think you are not particularly interested in the topics they teach.

Incidentally, if you want to take a course but don't have the prerequisites, you may be able to persuade the professor to waive them. If the professor sees you're interested and thinks you can do the work, you may have a shot.

Adding and Dropping Courses

So you made a mistake. Debra dropped Chinese Imaginative Literature (given in Chinese) and signed up for Shakespeare 101.

Most colleges have a procedure so you can change your mind about taking a course. In some schools, you register for courses first. Then you have a couple of weeks to assess the level of difficulty, the professor, and the content of the classes and decide if you want to continue. In other schools, there's a "shopping period" during which you can audit classes to determine whether or not you want to register. You may find out that you are way ahead of the other students in Conversational Italian. You may discover you have absolutely no idea what's going on in Astronomy of the Solar System. And you may be just plain bored out of your skull in Adolescent Development.

If you do register for a class and find out you've made a mistake—the professor is now reading all her lectures from the textbook she wrote, or the classes are all being taught by unprepared teaching assistants, or you can't keep up—you can usually bail out without penalty within the first few weeks. But remember—

you may be closed out from the course you'd like to take because it's full.

Josh, a sophomore at Ohio State, was overwhelmed by the number and variety of courses offered. His advice: "Trust yourself. It does take time to figure out priorities, but you will."

Learning How to Learn

The reading list for your history course contains more titles than all the books you read during your whole senior year in high school. Three papers are due the week before Thanksgiving. The chemistry instructor gives a quiz every Friday. You've only been there three weeks and you already have the sense that you are falling behind.

There's always too much to do, and part of what a freshman learns is what to do first, what to do next, and what to leave out. "I'm still finding out about things I can do and different avenues to make things easier," said a junior at the University of Mississippi. "It takes longer than you expect, but by your sophomore year you have a handle on things."

Reading

Everyone reads more than they ever did before, but some courses involve more reading than others. At college, the emphasis is on interpretation rather than memorization. As you read, it helps to get an overall feel for the material by scanning the assigned pages, noting bold face type, headings, and topic sentences. If there's a chapter summary or a list of review questions at the end, read them first. They will give you a good idea of the salient points—the ones most likely to turn up on a test.

It's a big help if you can read quickly. Reading specialists have proved that faster readers absorb more information and have a higher rate of comprehension than slower ones.

If you think you are reading too slowly, try to force yourself to move your eyes over the page faster than you normally do. You'll find this a little uncomfortable because you'll feel as if you're missing something. Put up with the frustration. Don't go back and reread. With practice, you'll find yourself skimming along at a faster clip.

Maybe you took a course to improve your reading speed before you came to college. If you didn't, it's worth doing early in your college career because this ability will help you in every aspect of your academic life and, later, out in the "real" world.

Speaking Up

Suppose, after a couple of weeks of Introduction to Contemporary Philosophy, you don't understand the lectures and you can never get through the reading. You feel as if you're drowning. Don't wait until you go down for the third time before stretching out a hand for help. The day before a paper is due or a big exam is scheduled is too late to go in and confess that you are totally lost.

Shyness pays no dividends. It's embarrassing to admit you don't understand something; however, the most direct way to find out what you need to know is to ask. Try raising your hand in class—you have nothing to lose but your ignorance. Besides, what makes you think you're the only student who's confused? Most teachers want to know when their message isn't getting through.

You don't have to be an anonymous student in a sea of freshman. There are ways to make personal contact, even in huge classes. You can try to get to know your instructor by arriving at class early or staying late for discussion. In virtually all colleges, instructors have office hours when you are welcome to come in and discuss the curriculum or any problems you may be having. Make an appointment. If you need more help than an office discussion can provide, your professor may be able to give you the name of someone who can tutor you through the rough spots.

"I would never have made it through Statistics—which I had to take—without help from my instructor and the graduate student who tutored me for a month," admitted Rheta, a psychology major at Franklin and Marshall.

Speaking up and asking for help made the crucial difference for Rheta. It will work for you, too.

Know Your Study Style

Manuel leaps out of bed as soon as his alarm buzzes. He's cheerful, he's wide awake, and he goes jogging around the lake. Then he comes back, reads for half an hour before breakfast, and bikes to class. He's never late. But by ten o'clock in the evening, he's a zombie.

Gerard never hears Manuel's alarm. He doesn't get up for breakfast, either. His conversation in the morning is limited to the occasional grunt. His memory of classes scheduled before ten o'clock is blurred. About two o'clock in the afternoon, Gerard really gets cooking, and at ten o'clock in the evening he's usually in the library.

Who sounds more like you? Do you recognize when you're revved up and when you're only spinning your wheels? It pays off if you can organize your schedule to mesh with your natural rhythms.

A major difference between high school and college is that in college most of your work will be done *outside* the classroom. You should expect to spend three or more hours of preparation for every hour you spend in class.

In high school, you probably did your homework every evening. In college, you will have more flexibility: Maybe Wednesday mornings are free, and that's the best time to hit the library for an uninterrupted couple of hours. If you're at your best after dinner, then that's when you should work on the term paper for History of Mass Communications (which your instructor has told you accounts for 50 percent of your final grade).

Where to Study

It should tell you something if you fall asleep every time you try to read propped up in bed. In order to study you should be comfortable, but not that comfortable!

Pick a place where you won't be interrupted and you can concentrate. This probably won't be the cafeteria during dining hours, the student lounge, the television room, or even your room, if there's too much going on. Libraries are designed for studying, and if you need an even more solitary setting, they have carrels—

small individual desk spaces, usually located in the stacks.

Some students can concentrate with headsets on, a TV in the corner, and people coming and going. Others require total silence and an empty room. You'll find the SOP—Study Operating Procedure—that works for you.

"When I used the library carrels, they were so quiet and isolated that I'd doze off," said Jay. "It was fine if I was writing a paper. But when I was just reading, I kept awake in the main reading room with other people around."

Taking Notes

You'll be taking two kinds of notes—notes on your reading and notes on what is said in the classroom.

Professors urge students to take notes while they're reading, to put the author's thoughts into their own words. Students generally limit themselves to the speedier techniques of highlighting or underscoring. Whatever your style, it'll stand you in good stead if you make a habit of reviewing your notes right after you've read the material.

In class, note-taking will help you stay focused. If you take good notes, kids who missed the class will seek you out and borrow them, which is another way to get to know new people. Ideally, your notes will remind you of the brilliant insights your professor brought to the subject, and give you a good idea of what you're likely to be tested on.

Professors have been known to put key points up on a chalkboard. Or, in the course of a lecture, they may say, "This is really important." These are serious hints, and you ignore them at your peril. "I do every-thing but send up a flare to alert my students to the major points I'm trying to get across," said a Boston University history professor. "It takes some of them a while to catch on, but they come to realize that when I say something's likely to appear on the exam, I'm not kidding."

Speedwriting and shorthand are good ways to take notes quickly, but you usually have to transcribe them and if you don't do so promptly, you may never figure out what you meant. If you'd like to tape a lecture, don't do so without first asking permission.

Students who go over their lecture notes the day they take them say it gives them a sense of security and satisfaction. Try it—you may like it.

Taking Tests

Usually, at the beginning of the semester, your profes-sor will tell you what tests you are in for and how they count toward your grade. Typically, there's at least a midterm and a final; however, there may be announced and unannounced quizzes and other exams as well.

Some students are great test takers. Others, even though they may know the material, don't react well to test pressure. However, if you cut a lot of classes and don't do the reading, you are definitely working on a scenario for academic failure.

Cramming your brains out in a last-minute study orgy may have worked in high school. And it may work for you in college—but it may not. You'll find out soon enough.

One comforting thought whenever you're feeling a little shaky about your ability to keep up academically: You did well enough in high school to get into college.

Most students do at least as well in college as they did in high school—and some do a whole lot better!

Learning to Use the Libraries

In today's college libraries, students are confronted with millions of books, thousands of magazines, and miles of microfiche, as well as an ever-increasing electronic data base. It's a different, more extensive, and more complicated world than the high school or neighborhood library.

Since the library will play a major role in your four years at college, the sooner you learn how to use it effectively, the better off you will be. Many college libraries offer an "Introduction to the Library" program—anything from a guided tour to an actual course. Take it as early as possible.

You'll learn the basics, such as how to use the card catalog or computer data base, and how to find the reference books, the copying machine, and the bathroom. Finding a librarian who knows the reference collection and is willing to help you is one of the wisest moves you can make.

If there are several libraries on campus, check them all out. The one with the books you need may not turn out to be the one you most like to work in.

"I was in premed, but I discovered that the law library was the best place to study," said Naomi, now a medical student at Einstein. "It was the quietest place, because law students have so much reading. Besides, it had wonderful wood paneling and extremely comfortable chairs."

If you don't get intimately acquainted with your college library in the first days, you surely will by the time your first research paper is due.

Scheduling Your Time

Winston is a first-semester freshman. He registered for freshman English seminar, Basic Biology (with a lab), Introduction to European History, and Social Psychology. He signed up to play for his dorm's basketball team, and he went to a meeting of the Parachute Club because he wants to jump out of airplanes. He auditioned for and got a part in the chorus of *Pirates of Penzance*. He has an on-campus job in the library, and is a member of the Afro-American Student Society.

Is Winston doing too much? Too little? Just enough?

It depends on his ability to manage his time. You've heard it before, and you'll hear it again: At college, you take charge of organizing your life.

Winston has to analyze his time commitments. School work comes first. Including his lab, he has approximately fifteen hours of classes. Figuring on three hours of studying and preparation per class hour, he's going to need about forty hours to keep up with his school work.

The dorm basketball team practices one afternoon a week and on Saturday mornings. Intramural games are usually played on Saturday afternoons. The Parachute Club convenes at a local airport on Saturday mornings and, weather permitting, stays there until everyone's had at least two jumps.

Chorus rehearsals are twice a week at first, and every evening for the two weeks before the show opens. Winston's library job involves spending two hours a day three days a week returning books to the shelves. The Afro-American Student Society meets on the third Thursday evening of each month.

Can Winston fit it all in? At first glance, his only problem seems to be that his extracurricular life has a couple of kinks in it. On Saturdays, he has to decide whether he wants to jump out of planes or shoot hoops, bearing in mind that if he makes a commitment to playing on a team, he'd better show up.

Rehearsals for *Pirates* are limited at first; however, will he be able to keep up with his studies when he has to be at the theater every evening?

You may think Winston's doing too much. But you'll probably find yourself doing the same kind of juggling, trying to balance what you have to do with what you want to do, and still finding time to party and hang out.

Write It Down

You can't possibly keep track of all you have to do unless you write it down. Students recommend a two-calendar system: one you hang on the wall or keep on the desk in your room, and the other you carry around with you. Write down when papers are due, exam dates, when the basketball team practices, and which weekend your cousin is coming to visit.

"In my very first class, the instructor said that a research paper would be due on the last day of the semester," says Phil, now a graduate student in Russian literature. "Once she approved my topic, she never mentioned the paper again, and I never gave it a thought until the week before it was due. It was a terrible shock! But I learned that nobody reminds you of anything—it's up to you."

Your calendar will help you spot free blocks of time, like the two hours between working in the library and your late-afternoon lab, so you can use them for homework and study. Try getting up an hour earlier. You'll be surprised at what you can accomplish.

Anybody can fritter time away. It's an art to learn how to do what has to be done in the time available. If there's not enough room on your calendar for everything you're supposed to do, you're probably doing too much!

Looking Ahead

So what are you going to be when you grow up?

Does this question tie your stomach in knots, or have you known since you were six that you wanted to be an astrophysicist?

One high school senior described her college nightmare: "I'll get to the end and I'll have a degree in nothing. I won't know what I want to do, or I'll spend four years on the wrong subject."

Freshmen have an inalienable right to worry about the future. However, four years is a long time. If you think about it in percentage terms, it's about 25 percent of your life so far! Think back to when you were a freshman in high school. You're not the same person today, any more than you will be four years from now when you graduate from college.

Many a would-be astrophysicist has learned that a childhood enthusiasm is not necessarily the basis for a lifelong career. Many "undecideds" discover an aptitude for research, a talent for technical writing, a passion for cultural anthropology—some previously unknown passion that leads them along unexpected and rewarding career paths.

Choosing a Major

Nobody wants you to declare a major right off the bat. Freshman year should be a breathing space, a time to ask yourself some of these questions:

☐ What do you enjoy doing?
☐ Do you like solving problems?
☐ Are you a leader?
☐ Do you prefer working alone or as part of a team?
☐ What are you good at?
☐ Have you ever taken an aptitude test?
☐ What really turns you on? Money? Fame? Power? Helping others?
☐ Do you have a strong geographic preference?

You won't find the answers to these questions at the back of this book! Figuring out who you are and what you want to do is an ongoing process that will continue far beyond your college years.

Many students—especially in economically depressed areas of the country—are realistically concerned about choosing a major that will lead to a job. Jerry Weber, a dean at the University of Oklahoma, noted that "Vocational focus is not new, but its influence on student choices cannot be overstated. Students today are less focused on questions of lifelong learning than was the student of years ago."

At some point, you may decide that your college career should lead directly to a specific kind of job. Or you may decide that your college years are a preparation for graduate school. But in your freshman year, you don't have to get obsessive about choosing your major. When the time comes, you'll find teachers, counselors, library resources, and professional materials to help you make an informed decision.

If it turns out you picked the wrong major, you can change direction. Switching majors is not a sign of immaturity or failure. If you're bored with your classes and doing poorly in key courses, you and your chosen field are mismatched. Don't confuse perseverance with obstinacy.

Taking Time Off

Your four years of college may expand to five or even six years, and you may not spend all of that time in one place. Some students take time off because they have to earn enough money to continue; others want a break and choose to spend a semester or two away.

Some study abroad or at another school. For example, Loyola University allows students to spend their junior year in Rome, and through a consortium arrangement students may cross-register for courses at Xavier and Tulane Universities and Notre Dame Seminary.

Some schools, such as Northeastern University, offer work-study programs and schedule a half-work, half-study academic year. At others, students take advantage of internships that give them firsthand work experience in various fields.

So while you're worrying about everything else, you can file these possibilities away for future reference.

A Vote of Confidence

You're in great shape. Your college knew what it was doing when it accepted you. Your teachers knew what they were doing when they recommended you. And your parents and friends are on your side.

You're going to sit through hundreds of classes and read mountains of books. You're going to write dozens of papers. And you're going to learn just as much, if not more, from all the people you're going to meet.

You're going to have an absolutely amazing time!

Appendix: What I Left Behind

As you look forward to starting your freshman year, it's hard to believe that it will come to an end. But it will.

What are you going to do with all the stuff you brought with you, plus all the stuff you accumulate?

You'll take some of it home with you, but there isn't much point in bringing your down jacket and your skis back for the summer. If you want to leave some stuff behind, most colleges do provide storage space. Or maybe you can leave it in a friend's apartment.

The big question is: Will you remember in September where you packed your belongings in May? To help you keep track, write down where you've left what.

What It Is	*Where It Is*
_____	_____
_____	_____
_____	_____
_____	_____
_____	_____
_____	_____
_____	_____
_____	_____
_____	_____
_____	_____
_____	_____
_____	_____
_____	_____

College Address Book
A–D

Name _____ Phone _____

Address _____

_____

Name _____ Phone _____

Address _____

_____

Name _____ Phone _____

Address _____

_____

Name _____ Phone _____

Address _____

_____

Name _____ Phone _____

Address _____

_____

Name _____ Phone _____

Address _____

_____

Name _____ Phone _____

Address _____

_____

College Address Book
E–K

Name ———————— Phone ————————
Address ——————————————————————————
——————————————————————————————————

Name ———————— Phone ————————
Address ——————————————————————————
——————————————————————————————————

Name ———————— Phone ————————
Address ——————————————————————————
——————————————————————————————————

Name ———————— Phone ————————
Address ——————————————————————————
——————————————————————————————————

Name ———————— Phone ————————
Address ——————————————————————————
——————————————————————————————————

Name ———————— Phone ————————
Address ——————————————————————————
——————————————————————————————————

Name ———————— Phone ————————
Address ——————————————————————————
——————————————————————————————————

College Address Book
L–R

Name _____ Phone _____

Address _____

_____

Name _____ Phone _____

Address _____

_____

Name _____ Phone _____

Address _____

_____

Name _____ Phone _____

Address _____

_____

Name _____ Phone _____

Address _____

_____

Name _____ Phone _____

Address _____

_____

Name _____ Phone _____

Address _____

_____

College Address Book
S–Z

Name _____ Phone _____

Address _____

_____

Name _____ Phone _____

Address _____

_____

Name _____ Phone _____

Address _____

_____

Name _____ Phone _____

Address _____

_____

Name _____ Phone _____

Address _____

_____

Name _____ Phone _____

Address _____

_____

Name _____ Phone _____

Address _____

_____

Notes

Other Books of Interest from
The College Board

Item #

002601 *Campus Visits and College Interviews,* by Zola Dincin Schneider. An "insider's" guide to campus visits and college interviews, including 12 checklists that will help students make the most of these firsthand opportunities.   ISBN: 0-87447-260-1, $9.95

002261 *The College Admissions Organizer.* This unique planning tool for college-bound students includes inserts and fill-in forms, plus 12 large pockets to store important admissions materials. ISBN: 0-87447-226-1, $16.95

002687 *The College Board Achievement Tests.* Complete and actual Achievement Tests given in 13 subjects, plus the College Board's official advice on taking the tests.   ISBN: 0-87447-268-7, $9.95

003101 *The College Board Guide to Preparing for the PSAT/NMSQT.* Contains four actual tests as well as practical test-taking tips, sample questions, and a comprehensive math review section.   ISBN: 0-87447-310-1, $8.95

002938 *The College Board Guide to the CLEP Examinations.* Contains nearly 900 questions from CLEP general and subject examinations, plus other information.   ISBN: 0-87447-293-8, $8.95

003152 *The College Cost Book, 1988–89.* A step-by-step guide to 1988–89 college costs, and detailed financial aid for 3,100 accredited institutions.   ISBN: 0-87447-315-2, $12.95 (Updated annually)

003136 *The College Handbook, 1988–89.* The College Board's official directory to more than 3,100 two-year and four-year colleges and universities.   ISBN: 0-87447-313-6, $16.95 (Updated annually)

002490 *College to Career,* by Joyce Slayton Mitchell. A guide to more than 100 careers, telling what the work is like, the education and personal skills needed, how many people are employed and where, and starting salaries and future employment prospects.   ISBN: 0-87447-249-0, $9.95

003055 *How to Help Your Teenager Find the Right Career,* by Charles J. Shields. Step-by-step advice and innovative ideas to help parents motivate their children to explore careers and find alternatives suited to their interests and abilities. ISBN: 0-87447-305-5, $12.95

002482 *How to Pay for Your Children's College Education,* by Gerald Krefetz. Practical advice to help parents of high school students, as well as of young children, finance their children's college education. ISBN: 0-87447-248-2, $12.95

003144 *Index of Majors, 1988–89.* Lists 500 majors at the 3,000 colleges and graduate institutions, state by state, that offer them. ISBN: 0-87447-314-4, $13.95 (Updated annually)

002911 *Profiles in Achievement,* by Charles M. Holloway. Traces the careers of eight outstanding men and women who used education as the key to later success. (Hardcover. ISBN: 0-87447-291-1, $15.95); 002857 paperback (ISBN: 0-87447-285-7, $9.95).

002598 *Succeed with Math,* by Sheila Tobias. A *practical* guide that helps students overcome math anxiety and gives them the tools for mastering the subject in high school and college courses, as well as the world of work. ISBN: 0-87447-259-8, $12.95

003039 *10 SATs: Third Edition.* Ten actual, recently administered SATs plus the full text of *Taking the SAT,* the College Board's official advice. ISBN: 0-87447-303-9, $9.95

002571 *Writing Your College Application Essay,* by Sarah Myers McGinty. An informative and reassuring book that helps students write distinctive application essays and explains what colleges are looking for in these essays. ISBN: 0-87447-257-1, $9.95

002474 *Your College Application,* by Scott Gelband, Catherine Kubale, and Eric Schorr. A step-by-step guide to help students do their best on college applications. ISBN: 0-87447-247-4, $9.95

To order by direct mail any books not available in your local bookstore, please specify the item number and send your request with a check made payable to the College Board for the full amount to: College Board Publications, Department M39, Box 886, New York, New York 10101-0886. Allow 30 days for delivery. An institutional purchase order is required in order to be billed, and postage will be charged on all billed orders. Telephone orders are not accepted, but information regarding any of the above titles is available by calling Publications Customer Service at (212) 713-8165.